MW00622924

WHAT IS LOVE?

WHAT IS LOVE?

Kyle Borg

GRASSMARKET PRESS
PITTSBURGH, PENNSYLVANIA

© 2022 Kyle Borg
Grassmarket Press

an imprint of
Crown & Covenant Publications
7408 Penn Avenue
Pittsburgh, PA 15208
crownandcovenant.com
All rights reserved.

Second printing, 2023

ISBN: 978-1-943017-57-7
eBook: 978-1-943017-58-4
Library of Congress Control Number: 2022944798

Printed in the United States of America

Theological editors of Grassmarket Press: Daniel Howe and Kyle Borg.

Text font is Minion Pro set in 11/15 point. Chapter titles are Mr Eaves XL Mod Nar OT. Interior and cover design by Esther Howe. Photograph of Grassmarket Square is from the Reformed Presbyterian Church of Scotland. Used by permission.

Scripture quotations are from the ESV® Bible (The Holy Bible, English Standard Version®), copyright © 2001 by Crossway, a publishing ministry of Good News Publishers. Used by permission. All rights reserved. The ESV text may not be quoted in any publication made available to the public by a Creative Commons license. The ESV may not be translated into any other language.

All rights reserved. No part of this book may be reproduced or stored in a retrieval system in any form by any means (electronic, mechanical, photocopying, recording or otherwise) without the prior written permission of the publisher.

To the Winchester Reformed Presbyterian Church whom I love, my joy and crown

CONTENTS

INTRODUCTION: A MAN OF LOVE

THERE ARE FEW MEN in the Bible as admired as David. His life and exploits capture the imagination of boys and grown men alike. That's because David had so many of the qualities that men value, and he connects with our idea of masculinity. I know for some people the word *masculinity* sounds toxic. Oh well. God created us male and female. That means there's a difference between men and women. We're different biologically, psychologically, and relationally, and that's okay. Actually, it's more than okay. The differences we see in the world around us are part of the Holy Spirit's wise ordering and beautifying of this present creation. And David stands out as a masculine man—even a man's man.

Our first introduction to David tells us a lot about him. The prophet Samuel came to David's father, Jesse. He was going to anoint one of Jesse's sons king of Israel. When Samuel arrived, he invited Jesse and his sons to meet him. Somehow, David either missed the message or wasn't included—he was off with the sheep. Samuel looked at Jesse's oldest son, Eliam, who was probably tall, strong, and maybe even had a commanding presence. Samuel thought that this must have been the Lord's chosen one. But God said to Samuel, "Do not look on his appearance or on the height of his stature, because I have rejected him. For the LORD sees not as man sees: man looks on the outward appearance, but the LORD looks on the heart" (1 Sam. 16:7).

As Samuel sized up the other sons of Jesse, the message was the same: "Not him." Not once, not twice, but seven times. Jesse had run out of sons! Well, not exactly. Samuel asked if there were any more, and Jesse said his youngest was keeping sheep. Someone went to fetch him and here's how we're first introduced to David: "Now he was ruddy and had beautiful eyes and was handsome" (1 Sam. 16:12). He wasn't as old, as tall, or as strong as his brothers, but he was the Lord's chosen one. God looks at the heart and not the outward appearance.

From that point in the story grows the biblical history of David. He gains the reputation of being "a man of valor, a man of war, prudent in speech, and a man of good presence"

(1 Sam. 16:18). When the armies of Israel—all their famed and seasoned warriors—shrank under the gleaming eye and verbal taunts of Goliath, it was David who stood alone on the battlefield and took the giant's head. His military conquests increased and he was celebrated as a man of renown: "Saul has struck down his thousands, and David his ten thousands" (1 Sam. 18:7). He conquered kingdoms, enforced justice, escaped the edge of the sword, became mighty in war, and put foreign armies to flight (Heb. 11:32–40). Eventually David took the throne of Israel, established their borders, and restored the worship of God.

That's impressive. If you're not familiar with the life of David, go read about it in the Old Testament books of 1 and 2 Samuel. Was he perfect? Not a chance! The Bible doesn't sugarcoat his epic failures—his epic sins. He sinned as a man, as a husband, as a father, and as a king. And there were terrible consequences. But remember, God looks at the heart. It's not the outward victories that make a man noble. Inwardly, David was a man of faith, humility, and repentance who didn't waver in the promises of God. It's for this reason that God himself declared David to be a man after his own heart (see 1 Sam. 13:14).

There's another inward quality of David, however, that deserves our attention. This man was a man of love. In some way, it might even be his defining quality. In fact, the name David actually means "beloved." He lived up to that name.

David was loved. The Bible says Saul loved him, and Saul's daughter Michal and son Jonathan loved him. Servants loved David, and all of Israel and Judah loved him. But he was also beloved by God, and as David was loved by God, he loved in return. Turn the pages of his history and you'll see it—he loved God, he loved his family, he loved his friends, and he even loved his enemies.

This didn't make him less of a man. Why? Well, it wasn't the kind of love you find scribbled in a Hallmark® greeting card or the feeble love of cupid and pierced hearts. It wasn't the kind of love that makes us feel a little (or maybe a lot) uncomfortable or effeminate. No, it was the kind of love that David's son Solomon said was as strong as death: "Its flashes are flashes of fire, the very flame of the LORD" (Song of Sol. 8:6). Or, as it could be read: "a lightning flash of the LORD."

That's quite the description! There is nothing weak or wimpy about that love. Step outside on a summer night as a storm rolls in. The display of lightning is amazing. It flashes for a split second, but in that second its light consumes all the darkness above and below. As quickly as it flashes, it disappears, leaving your unadjusted eyes to be momentarily blind even in the darkness. Such brilliance. Such intensity. Such force and power. What is love? It's that. It's more than that. Forget the lighting of the clouds. It's the lightning flash of the Lord—a fire of supernatural power kindled by God himself—and it burns and melts with unquenchable intensity.

We need people with that kind of love. Well, to be fair, our world is in desperate need for men of faith, strength, courage, wisdom, and humility. They're in short supply! But like branches of a tree, these things grow from the trunk of love. We need those who know the lightning flash of the Lord. We need men and women who are deeply beloved by God and love in return. This is what our spouses need. It's what our children and grandchildren need. It's what your church, friends, and society need from you. So, I invite you to read and to hear me out. Give me sixteen chapters (and a quick conclusion) to tell you about the lightning flash of the Lord.

1

THE VOICES OF LOVE

LOVE. IT'S A FOUR-LETTER WORD. No, not the kind of four-letter word that got your mouth washed out with soap. It's simply a word with four letters. The longest word in an English dictionary has forty-five letters. I doubt you've heard it. I hadn't! I had to look it up. Apparently, it's a technical word for a lung disease. It makes sense that something as complicated as lung disease would have a complicated name both in its spelling and pronunciation. But *love* isn't a word like that. It's not an obscure word found at the bottom of a pile of research known to a select few who have fancy initials after their names. It's simple. It's everywhere. It's part of our daily vocabulary. It's the combination of two consonants and two vowels: l-o-v-e.

But love itself isn't simple. Behind those four letters is something (let's call love a "something" for now) that's complicated. Maybe we think it shouldn't be. Someone once told me it isn't. They said when you find the right person to love it comes naturally. As a husband, dad, pastor, and friend, I think they lied, or, at least, they didn't know what they were talking about. Love isn't easy. Love has to do with our needs, emotions, experiences, desires, and relationships. Love is deeply embedded in what it means to be human—both for men and women. So, if you're a human being you should probably have some idea of what this "something" we call love is. It seems to me, however, anyone who begins to think (much less write) about love will agree with C. S. Lewis, who wrote in *The Four Loves*: "The reality is more complicated than I supposed."

So where do I start? I'm going to begin by telling you how you think about love. I know, it's a gutsy move! After years of marriage, I still make the mistake of telling my wife what she thinks. Can I really know what *you* think about love? Chances are I've never met you, so how can I? But hear me out before you shout me down saying, "Don't tell me what I think!" My basic assumption is that your idea of love didn't spring up from nowhere. There's a fun Latin phrase for that: *ex nihilo*—out of nothing. Your idea of love isn't *ex nihilo*. It's not spontaneous. It's not creative. It's probably not very personal. What if I said most of your ideas of love came from someone telling you what your idea of love should be?

When I was in basic training there was a guy in my flight—that's what a training group is called in the Air Force—who was a loud mouth. He thought he knew everything. I remember my sergeant (no kidding, his name was Sergeant Dye) putting the smart aleck in his place. He yelled in his face: "If I want *your* opinion, *I'll* give it to *you*." Wait a second. That's not how opinions are supposed to work. *I'm* supposed to tell *you* what *my* opinion is. But that's my point. Someone has given you your opinion of love. Actually, it's probably lots of someones. I'm convinced you have a lot of voices around you saying: "This is what *your* opinion of love is." But don't think of yourself as a helpless victim. We're all too happy to listen to the voices. We practically beg them to feed us our opinions.

But don't take it from me. Every harebrained idea should be supported by quoting someone. It's even better if that someone is dead. The living? They're okay. Use them when necessary, but do it sparingly. But if you can quote the dead, for whatever reason people find it easier to believe. So let me tell you that this observation isn't my own. In fact, Francois de la Rouchefoucauld (can you imagine learning how to spell that in kindergarten?) said almost the same thing. Rouchefoucauld was famous in his day for writing "maxims." A maxim is a short saying. Basically, he mastered the art of Twitter 300 years before Twitter did! One of his maxims was this: "There are some who never would have loved if they never had heard of love."

Still skeptical? Let's stop and listen for a moment to one of the voices who has given you your opinion of love. I studied philosophy in college. I'm not sure it made me a lover of wisdom (that's what "philosophy" means) but it's kind of fun telling people I majored in wisdom! One of the biggest things I learned was that most of us are like a trout swimming in a stream. Unless that trout makes the determined effort to swim against the current, it is swept along by it. Yep, I spent tens of thousands of dollars to learn that analogy. There are some systems of thoughts and ideas that flow through our culture like a river current. Unless we do the difficult work of swimming against that current, we're probably swept along with it.

This is true about your idea of love. In the history of humanity, people haven't always thought the same way about love. Simple test case: when most of us hear "love" we have a natural inclination to think of romantic love. That's the love we prioritize, and finding it brings fulfillment. It was different for Aristotle. Aristotle was a Greek philosopher who lived more than 2,300 years ago. If you would have asked Aristotle about love, he wouldn't have thought about romantic love, but rather he would have immediately thought of friendship.

Back to my main point—humanity hasn't always thought of love in the same way, and the way that most of us think about it is strongly influenced by a movement called Romanticism. Let me piece together a few things. Romanticism did well in the late 18th to mid-19th centuries. It's difficult to give a simple definition for Romanticism, but it altered the way many people understand and express themselves. Romanticism arose in the shadow of the Industrial Revolution: a revolution characterized by faceless grinding machinery, sort of a dull and dreary take on reality. Romanticism broke from that by emphasizing things like the individual, the emotion, the subjective, and the imagination. While it impacted art, literature, politics—really, everything—it also gave a new way to think about love. And what kind of love? Namely, romantic love between two people.

ROSE-COLORED GLASSES

According to Aaron Ben-Ze'ev and Ruthama Goussinsky in their book *In the Name of Love*, the basic traits of Romanticism's definition of love centered on love's profundity, the uniqueness of the one you love, and love's purity. What does that mean? Stick with me! Profundity means we became convinced that romantic love is the most significant love and has an ability to continue forever and ever. Think about every fairy-tale ending: "They lived happily ever after." Uniqueness means we view the one we love as being irreplaceable. They are, after all, supposed to be "the one." Finally, purity means that love is and can only be good. These basic traits continue to shape the way we think about love.

Maybe at this point you're rolling your eyes thinking this is a bunch of mumbo-jumbo. After all, you don't read romance books! But this idea of love between two people—its profundity, uniqueness, and purity—began to fill novels, poetry, music, and art. As it did, it began to tell people what their opinion—their description and definition—should be. And it was a powerful influence. It was observed in *Gentleman's Magazine* in 1907:

> Of all the earthly artillery which love has employed to brighten eyes, and soften hearts, the most effectual and forcible is the modern novel. Of all the arrows which Cupid has shot at youthful hearts this is the keenest. There is no resisting it. It is the literary opium, that lulls every sense into delicious rapture.

Opium, that's a drug right? The point is, like a highly addictive drug, this idea of love caught on. As Ben-Ze'ev said: "We yearn to experience the idealized love depicted in so many novels, movies, poems, and popular songs."

Let me give you some practical examples. Think of the fairy-tale ending, "happily ever after." Did you know that this expression likely came about in the 18th century as a result of . . . Romanticism? Have you been convinced that there is one person out there who is your soulmate? That, too, is Romanticism. Think about those consoling words often spoken to the brokenhearted: "If it's meant to be, it will happen." Guess what? Romanticism. Turn the volume up a bit on the Beatles' iconic song "All You Need is Love," and you'll be listening to the melody of Romanticism. Add to this the idea of love at first sight, love's ability to overcome any obstacle, butterflies in the stomach, and sex as the greatest expression of love. Yes, you're right, Romanticism, Romanticism, Romanticism, and Romanticism. As Alain de Botton said in a superb talk (helpful to the preceding paragraphs) he gave at the Sydney Opera House in Australia: "You are influenced, because we all are, by Romanticism."

Romanticism provides the rose-colored glasses through which most of us have come to view love. But it's not the way that human history has always viewed it. If you were to sit at a table and discuss love with the Ancient Greeks, for instance, many of the above sentiments would be unknown to them. Of course, that's not saying much. Many of the Greeks thought the highest love—what they called heavenly love—was a love between a man and a boy that we, even today in our highly sexualized and progressive culture, still consider taboo. Seriously, go pick up Plato's *Symposium*. But my point is this: your idea of love isn't much your own.

It's been given to you by many voices, and one of those is philosophy.

VOICES IN YOUR HEAD

But philosophy isn't the only voice. You could easily add other voices: psychology, sociology, biology, economics, politics, and even mathematics. That's right, mathematics! No joke, mathematicians have actually tried to discover the formula of love. Personally, I'm still working on subtraction—I don't need to mathematically figure out love. But everyone, literally everyone, is saying something about love. Let's stop and listen to what some of the voices have said and are saying.

Listen to the way personality tests have influenced your idea of love. Popular tests such as Myers-Briggs or Enneagram assign letters or numbers to an individual to explain their compatibility in romance and friendships, and they also try to tell us how we show and receive love. Or think of the way scientists have studied the brain trying to understand the biochemical foundations of love or mapping out basic drives like the sex drive or the desire for long-term attachment.

Consider the voices that express traditional ideas of masculinity and femininity, defining what is or is not an appropriate expression of love, and the voices that challenge those traditions. Is it okay for a man to tell another man "I love you" without there being an erotic assumption? My grandfather told me when I was a boy that men don't hug as a way to express even family love, but rather we should shake hands. Listen to the voices of politics where legislatures and judges try to determine the boundaries of marriage, which they describe as the "highest ideal of love," or the way a former president nonsensically declared: "Love is love." Listen to the way the economy sells us our idea of love with chocolates, roses, and stuffed bears. Listen to the way literature—the stuff we were forced to read in high school—in its prose, poetry, and plays centers on the theme of love gained and lost in all its various relationships. We've immortalized Romeo and Juliet, and women long for their own Mr. Darcy. And roses are still red, and violets are still blue.

Maybe the loudest voice around us today is pop culture. Much of what we think about love is learned and reinforced by Hollywood. Movies and television give us a standard of expectation for our relationships. Never mind how unattainable or unrealistic it is; it gives us an ideal to strive for. Music has long touched the nerve center of our emotions and informed and shaped our opinions and expressions of love, from the innocence of the Golden Oldies to the love ballads of the '80s to the trashy anthems of today. Social media continues to stretch our understanding of categories like friendship, connection, and companionship. The porn industry has drastically altered (and ruined!) our ideas of romance, intimacy, desire, and affection. Seriously! The fact that generations have formed their idea of love from porn stars who (male or female) are glorified prostitutes is a tragedy from which we will not soon recover. If that characterization offends you more than the influence they have over young hearts, I don't know what to tell you.

Our idea of love is influenced by what we listen to, read, and watch. These are the voices that are all around, and they merge together to yell in our faces: "If I want your opinion of love, I'll give it to you!" Don't be mistaken. This idea of love that these voices give us isn't a small matter. Our idea of love is powerful. People live for it, kill for it, and die for it. Love motivates acts of courage and bravery. It storms battlefields and wins wars. It protects and defends. It nurtures and heals. It takes and it gives. On November 21, 2010, Marine Corporal Kyle Carpenter threw himself onto a grenade to try to save the life of his friend Nick Eufrazio. He suffered catastrophic wounds. When he received the Congressional Medal of Honor, the president said that the heroic act fulfilled those words: "Greater love hath no man than this; that a man lay down his life for his friends."

But love's power can also be dangerous. I read a news story recently about a man who was convicted of murder. He stabbed a woman fourteen times. Why? Because he loved her. Pause. He did that in the name of love? Yep! Somewhere and somehow he got the wrong idea of love. He'll spend the rest of his life in prison because his love isn't love, it's hate. In 2002, Thad Roberts hatched a plan to steal moon rocks from NASA. He successfully pulled off the heist, stealing $21 million worth of rocks, but was soon arrested. His motive? He'd fallen in love with an intern named Tiffani, and he wanted to give her the moon. You can't make this up! In 2013, Jose Magana-Farias was arrested for falsely imprisoning his ex-wife and trying to perform an exorcism on her so she would love him again. In 2019, fashion designer Mossimo Giannulli and actress Lori Loughlin were arrested and charged in a college admissions scandal. For love, they illegally bribed their daughters' way into college. It's catastrophic but many parents do things for their children in the name of love!

What a difference! We praise and award a Marine for his love, and we condemn others for theirs. Why? Because deep down we know that love isn't all we need. We also need to love *well.* We need to love *rightly*. So who gets to define that? Which voice is worth listening to, and which voices should be ignored? Is philosophy right? Is psychology right? Sociology? Biology? Politics? Economics? Literature? Hollywood? Music? Social media? Porn? Who gets to tell you what love is?

In the midst of these noisy voices, we need a louder voice. We need a voice that can break through the chatter and clearly, authoritatively, conclusively define for us what love is. It's a definition that doesn't depend on culture, place, or time. It's not like a set of clothes that goes in and out of style. Maybe there was a hint of truth when Shakespeare wrote of love's unchanging character in Sonnet 116:

> Love's not Time's fool, though rosy lips and cheeks
> Within his bending sickle's compass come;
> Love alters not with his brief hours and weeks,
> But bears it out even to the edge of doom.

It's the goal of this book to get you to listen to a better voice: *the voice of God*. It's the voice of God *who is love*. It's the voice of God who is love, *and he has spoken in the Bible.*

2

LOVE ISN'T GOD

DURING THE SPRING of my sophomore year of college, I had to take Logic 101. It was miserable. Not only because it was, according to campus rumors, the most-failed class at the university—right alongside statistics—but because of the professor. None of the experienced professors in the department liked teaching the class, and so it usually fell to that semester's student teacher who wasn't good at teaching. In fact, he was the first full-grown adult I ever witnessed throwing a temper tantrum. Trying to solve a problem on the board, he kept getting the wrong answer, and a student finally chimed in and asked, "Why are we paying you to teach us?" He threw his dry erase marker across the room, stomped his feet, and yelled, "I don't need to know how to do logic to pass this class, *you do*!"

Although logic can lead to frustrations—for teachers and students alike—it's important. Whether we're aware of it or not we use logic every day. If the weatherman says, "Today it's going to rain," you're likely to grab an umbrella on your way out the door to stay dry. Why? Because it's logical! Of course, if the weatherman says, "Today is going to be sunny without a cloud in the sky," you'd look like a fool to bring an umbrella with you. Why? Because it's illogical! In the last chapter, I called love a "something." If we're going to listen to what the voice of the Bible says about this something, we'll need to keep a basic rule of logic in mind.

OUR STARTING POINT

The apostle John was one of Jesus's disciples. He was with Jesus for most of his three years of ministry. Many believe he was the youngest of the men that followed Jesus, and according to the New Testament, he was "the one whom Jesus loved" (John 20:2). It's also believed that he outlived the other apostles, and late in life, even as a very old man, he wrote a significant part of the New Testament—the Gospel of John, three letters, and the book of Revelation.

It's from the pen of John that we receive some of the clearest biblical teaching on love. John loved love, and he loved to write about it. If we want to understand what love is, then we need to begin with one of the most important things John ever wrote: "God is love" (1 John 4:8). That's our starting point.

But here is where we need to remember a little logic. In saying "God is love," we need to be careful not to get things backward. I recently saw a protest on the news. In the crowd of people, a number of signs were being held up. One of the signs—in big bold red letters—said: "God = Love and Love = God." I have no doubt that in the mind of the smiling person holding the sign were the words of John: "God is love." Unfortunately, well-intentioned as I'm sure that person was, they failed to understand a little bit of logic.

It's one thing to say "God is love," and it's another to say "love is God." Do you see the difference? Let me give you an example. If I said, "A dad is a male," that would be true. In the God-made differences between men and women, being a dad is something that only a male can be (and being a mom is something only a female can be). But, let's reverse that and say, "A male is a dad." Is that true? No. My son is a male, and at ten years old, he isn't a dad. You see there's a difference between saying "a dad is a male" and "a male is a dad." So, too, with what John writes. We can't just willy-nilly reverse the order and say, "Love is God."

Is this a point that needs to be made? Yes. We live in a day that has reversed the equation. Rather than saying with the apostle John, "God is love," our culture declares, "Love is god" (yes, I mean that with a lowercase "g"). The fallout of this backwards logic is massive. Let's think about it.

A "god"—broadly defined—can be thought of as someone or something that is absolute and authoritative and so demands our highest allegiance. Even though atheism and agnosticism seem cool in our culture, we're actually really good at crowning and enthroning gods in our lives. No person can escape having a god. That's because there's an impulse in the human heart to want something to rally around, something to trust in, something to depend on—even something to throw wholehearted commitment and service behind.

For example, some people make money their god. It's the most important thing in their life, and it's what they live for. They may have ditched the God of the Bible, but the throne doesn't sit empty. They just shove dollar signs onto it, and they're willing to sacrifice all their time, energy, and even their families to make money. Others do the same with pleasure. Happiness is all that they live for, and they do whatever makes them happy. How many times have you heard "As long as it makes you happy?" If that's how you live you might as well admit it: happiness is your god. We could add to these examples—science, politics, sex, entertainment, possessions, work, family, and so on. In fact, the apostle Paul even says some people make their belly their god (Phil. 3:19). Even the staunchest atheist makes a god of something or someone.

That's exactly what many people do with love: "Love is god." Love, whatever it is, is the absolute and authoritative thing that demands unquestioning allegiance. Now, I get it. There's a certain appeal to that. At least people aren't saying "Selfishness is god" or "Anger is god." If they're going to enthrone something, at least it's something that sounds nice. But there's a big problem. *If* love is god, what is love?

WHAT IS IT?

Now we're right back at the problem of the first chapter. Everyone around you has an idea of love. But if "love is god," that doesn't *only* mean everyone has a definition, it also means their idea of love is enthroned. I've already mentioned it, but it's worth picking on further. After the Supreme Court ruling that found a constitutional right for same-sex marriage in the United States, President Barack Obama helped popularize the phrase "Love is love." It's nonsensical, but it packs a punch. It sounds like it makes sense. But alas, the emperor has no clothes! It's babble. Love is self-defining. Love is ultimate. Love is all-controlling. Love is god, and it requires only submission.

But, to be clear, when President Obama said, "Love is love," he didn't mean "*your* idea of love is love." He actually meant "*My* idea of love is love." And if "love is god," that means everyone and anyone must give unquestioning allegiance to my idea of love. Well, to be more accurate, they must give unquestioning allegiance to *me*. That creates a dangerous world. It creates a world where everyone is a demigod. As we've seen it play out in society and in people's daily lives, any opposition to the thought "My idea of love is god" must be silenced or canceled entirely.

Let's go a step further. If "love is god" that also means that not just our neighbor but God himself is held accountable to my idea of love. As a Christian and as a pastor, I often hear people say, "If God is loving, then he can't do X, Y, or Z." The X, Y, or Z usually has to do with some of the more difficult things we read about God in the Bible: judgment, destruction, and death. Some time ago I was talking to a young man who had given up Christianity. When I asked him why, he told me it was because of what the Bible taught about hell—that it's eternal punishment for those who don't believe the gospel of Jesus Christ. He argued this way: "If God is loving then he can't punish someone forever." I pushed back a little "Why not?" He went on to explain that the whole idea of hell was unloving. Do you see what he did? Don't be fooled! He made love to be god over God. To put it simply, his idea of love is the absolute authority, and even God must bend the knee because love is god.

Of course, this is just one or two examples. But people do this all the time. They have made love god. Maybe you're okay with that. Maybe you're willing to accept the fallout from that—a society full of demigods demanding everyone bend the knee to their idea of love. Maybe you're okay. But I'll bet if push came to shove you wouldn't be. That's because you know and I know that not every definition of love is equal. Even by society's measurement, some definitions are outright wicked and perverse.

So, let's not start with "love is god." Let's start with what John does say. John starts with God, and the one who is God *is love*. Let's start there and see where that will take us. Let's see if the Bible can give us a better definition, indeed the best definition, of what love is.

3

GOD IS LOVE

I HOPE YOU DON'T MIND if I repeat myself. I grew up learning that if you repeat something to yourself at least three times you have a better chance of remembering it. So, I'll go ahead and do it and won't ask forgiveness. In the first chapter, I pointed out that whether we're aware of it or not there are a lot of voices in the world around us giving us our definition of love. What is needed? A louder voice. Namely, the voice of God in the Bible. In the second chapter, we took as our starting point the apostle John's simple phrase: "God is love." But somehow many people have failed logic class and turned that around to mean "love is god." That most certainly is not what John meant when he wrote those words. So what did he mean? Let's figure it out.

THE NATURE OF GOD

First, "God is love" means that love is the nature of God. Don't get too confused. The word *nature* and other words like it such as *essence* and *being* can be complicated. Basically, something's nature is what that something *is*. When John writes "God is love," he's saying that's what God is, *he is love*. With God, love isn't something he's fallen into, it's not an activity he's engaged in, and it's not a relationship that came into existence when he first said, "Let there be light." In his being—which the Bible tells us is infinite, eternal, and unchangeable—*he is love*.

But wait! Let me hit the pause button. I don't want you to misunderstand this. While it's true that God is love, we need to know that this isn't all the Bible says God is. John didn't write (and none of the biblical authors do), "God is *only* love." This isn't a book on the attributes of God, so I'll let someone else write that. But saying "God is love" doesn't deny that he is also wise. The apostle Paul wrote, "Oh, the depth of the riches and wisdom and knowledge of God! How unsearchable are his judgments and how inscrutable his ways!" (Rom. 11:33). Saying "God is love" doesn't mean he isn't holy. The prophet Isaiah heard the winged creatures in heaven crying out: "Holy, holy, holy is the Lord of hosts" (Isa. 6:3). Saying "God is love" doesn't mean he isn't also just. Moses spoke of him, saying, "A God of faithfulness and without iniquity, just and upright is he" (Deut. 32:4). It also doesn't mean that God isn't merciful, gracious, patient, and true. God *is* all those things and even more.

It also doesn't mean that love is at the center of who God is and all these other things are on the sidelines. Sometimes, even well-meaning people think that. I heard someone say once, "Yes, God is just but he's really and truly loving." But that isn't how it works. You see, what God is and all that he is, *he is*. Whew! Let me write that again. What God is and all that he is, *he is*.

I remember when I was in high school and my dad took us on a fly fishing trip to Colorado. We rented a Jeep Wrangler, did some off-roading, and found ourselves high in the mountains at a secluded lake to do some excellent trout fishing. Before going, we were warned that we would need to be careful how much we exerted ourselves. The oxygen was thinner on the mountaintop than at the base, and we were assured it would be a little harder to breathe. Well, it's easy when we talk about the attributes of God this way to quickly climb heights where it's a little harder to breathe. This is one of those places.

All that God is, he is. That means that none of God's attributes are distinct from who he is. For example, I have four daughters. One of them is nearing teenage years and with it, her opinion of me is . . . well, let's just say Dad isn't quite what he used to be. But, if you asked my youngest daughter to describe me, I hope she'd say, "My dad is strong, smart, handsome, and funny." Okay. It's just an example. She has a personality a lot like mine, so I suspect she'd make one big joke out of me, but let's pretend that's what she said. She isn't saying that being handsome is identical to being me. Being strong, smart, or funny are just parts of what make me me. But none of them *is* me.

It's different when we think about God. God doesn't only *possess* goodness, power, justice, or love. God *is* those things—he is his attributes. All that God is, God is. Remember Moses? Moses was tending a flock one day in the wilderness when he saw a bush on fire. What was peculiar about this bush is that it was on fire but unburned. As he approached the bush, a voice spoke to him. It's one of the most well-known scenes in the whole Bible. During his encounter, Moses asked the one who was speaking what his name was. What was the response? "God said to Moses, 'I AM WHO I AM'" (Exod. 3:14). God named himself. And he named himself in this strange way—*he is who he is.*

Every quality of God is identical to who he is. That means, like I've said above, we shouldn't think of God's love as the center of who he is and everything else—his justice, goodness, wisdom, truth—as sitting on the sidelines. Or, if it helps to think of food, God's love isn't 50% of the pie while the other attributes get to split the other 50%. Not at all. Love isn't more important or higher or bigger or more real than the other qualities of God. All that is in God is God.

THE RELATIONSHIPS IN GOD

Second, "God is love" means something more. Even before God created all things, he was involved in a relationship of love. How is that possible? It's possible because even though God is one in nature, the Bible tells us that he is three in person—Father, Son, and Holy Spirit. Just like this isn't a book about the attributes of God, it's also not a book about the Trinity. I will leave that subject to someone else as well. But it does have a place here when we think about "God is love."

C. S. Lewis once wrote that saying "God is love" has no meaning unless there's at least two persons in God. Why? Because to love requires one who loves and one who is loved. While there's probably room to argue with Lewis a little bit, his point is still helpful. God's love doesn't depend on his creation. Or, to put it another way, the love of God didn't come into existence when everything else did. That's because Christianity is centered on the triune God. God is one. He has a single nature. The one God is three in person. The Father isn't the Son, the Son isn't the Spirit, and the Spirit isn't the Father. But there aren't three Gods, there is only one God.

This helps us, in part, to understand what "God is love" means. That's because the Father, Son, and Spirit have eternally existed in a relationship of love. One day in college when I was walking to class, I was reading a book. For the record, that's not a habit I would recommend. It's very hard to pay attention to the sidewalk while you're also trying to read. But I suppose, nowadays everyone has a smartphone, so I'm sure my caution will fall on deaf ears. As I was reading, I came across a sentence that absolutely stunned me: "God loves himself supremely." That was something I had never heard before, and it can be staggering the first time you read it. But it's true.

We need to be careful to try to understand things that are beyond our understanding. For example, John writes, "In this the love of God was made manifest among us, that God sent his only Son into the world" (1 John 4:9). Why does that Father's gift of sending his Son into the world show his love? It's because the Father loves his Son and he has loved him since before the foundation of the world (see John 3:35, 5:20, and 17:24). Even if God had never created the world, he would still be the God who is love.

THE SOURCE OF LOVE

Finally, "God is love" expresses something else. Is God's nature love? Yes. In his own inter-trinitarian relationships, does God love? Yes. Are those somewhat hard to understand? Probably. But there's something perhaps a little simpler: he's also the source of all love. He is a God who has chosen to show his love to sinful people. He shows his love in forgiveness: "Turn, O LORD, deliver my life; save me for the sake of your steadfast love" (Ps. 6:4). In his mercy: "Have mercy on me, O God, according to your steadfast love" (Ps. 51:1). In his comfort: "Let your steadfast love comfort me" (Ps. 119:76). And it endures forever: "The steadfast love of the Lord never ceases; his mercies never come to an end" (Lam. 3:22).

The love of God is shown most in Jesus Christ. John wrote: "For God so loved the world that He gave His only begotten Son" (John 3:16). The sending of his only Son into the world is the greatest demonstration of love imaginable—it's self-giving in the greatest sense. The Father has sent the Son into the world to die in the place of sinners so that through faith in Jesus we might have forgiveness and life. One old preacher named Octavius Winslow once asked: "Who delivered up Jesus to die? Not Judas for money; not Pilate, for fear; not the Jews, for envy;—but the Father, for love." To put it simply, anyone who knows God through Jesus has found him to be a God of love—infinite and boundless love.

As we come to know the God who is love through faith in Jesus, that actually creates love in us for him and others. Here's what John writes:

> Beloved, let us love one another, for love is from God, and whoever loves has been born of God and knows God. Anyone who does not love does not

> know God, because God is love. In this the love of God was made manifest among us, that God sent his only Son into the world, so that we might live through him. In this is love, not that we have loved God but that he loved us and sent his Son to be the propitiation for our sins. (1 John 4:7–10)

If we're going to hear God's voice in helping us to understand what love is, this is where we must start. We must start where John starts: *God is love.*

4

THE EXCELLENCY OF LOVE

I STILL REMEMBER THE DAY I was in the parking lot with my son helping him get his football gear strapped on. I plopped his helmet on his head and said, as I usually do, "Have a good game. Play hard. I love you." Self-consciousness got the better of him. Fearful someone might overhear him, he nodded his head and said, "Thanks." That was it. My "I love you" was met with his "Thanks." That was the first time since he had learned to talk that he didn't say the words back to me. Of course, the apple doesn't fall far from the tree, and many young men can remember those moments with their own dad. I suspect almost every guy has been there.

I sometimes wonder if this is part of the cultural baggage we have to lug around when it comes to love. Boys imagine being and doing all kinds of things when they grow up. They want to be athletic and excel in sports. They want to be handy with tools or know their way around a car engine. They want survival and outdoor skills. Or they want to get a college degree. Boys want to be tough, brave, confident, respected, and ambitious. They want their legacy to be greatness. None of these things are bad, and they are indeed worthy pursuits. The world needs more men like that. But how many boys want to grow up to be a man of love? I haven't met one yet.

I'm not exactly sure why. Maybe it's because somewhere in our cultural understanding and expression of love, love isn't manly. Robert Moore and Douglas Gillette wrote in their book *King, Warrior, Magician, Lover* that "in the late twentieth century, we face a crisis in masculine identity of vast proportions."

Maybe this is the fruit of that crisis. After all, love is often depicted in feminine ways. Don't believe me? Go look at the Hallmark® rack of cards and try to find one that communicates love in a masculine way. Or, at other times, love is reduced to an emotionalism or sentimentality that doesn't connect well with men. It may leave girls fawning at the latest chick-flick but what guy wants to be *that*? Maybe it's because we've so sexualized love that straight men feel moderately gay even expressing the word. Like I said, I don't know. But it's too bad.

THE BEST WAY

It's too bad because love really is an excellent thing. That's how the apostle Paul phrased it. Let's see, how would I describe Paul? Paul was a brilliant scholar. He had studied the Old Testament and the Jewish traditions far beyond any layperson. He was well acquainted with culture and the culture's influencers. He also hated the church. In fact, he watched as Christians were killed and did his best to have them imprisoned. At least he did until he met the ascended Lord Jesus on the road to Damascus and was blinded by his glory. God, in his grace, turned Paul's life around and made him a servant. In his service to Jesus, Paul lived a hard life—a very hard life. He was often jailed, got beat up a lot, and was often near death. He was whipped, beaten with rods, and stoned. He was shipwrecked, adrift at sea, and in danger in the city and in the wilderness. I imagine his body was bent over in pain and bore the scars of his many wounds. Brilliant and battered may be the best way to describe him.

But Paul knew the excellency of love. In one of his letters, he wrote to the church in Corinth—that church was a hot mess. One of their biggest problems was that they were a very talented church. By "talented" I mean they were a church with a lot of spiritual gifts given by the Holy Spirit. That's a good thing. Unfortunately, the Corinthians took a good thing and used it in a bad way. These gifts had made them proud, arrogant, and rude toward one another. So this brilliant and battered man had to write and set them straight.

What did they need to hear? They needed to hear that their spiritual gifts were good. That's because they were given by the Spirit of God for the benefit of the church. But more than wanting the gifts, Paul wrote and said, "I will show you a still more excellent way" (1 Cor. 12:31). The word for "excellent" is a word that means *throwing beyond others*. In other words, as great as their gifts were, Paul is saying he's going to show them something that goes beyond gifts—not only *an* excellent way but the *most* excellent way. The best way of all. And that is the way of love.

BETTER THAN THE LAW OF THE JUNGLE

Ernest Gordon was an officer in the Argyll and Sutherland Highlanders during World War II. After the capture of Singapore he, with some other British officers, tried to escape to Sri Lanka on a fishing boat. Unfortunately, they were captured by the Japanese. He was sent as a prisoner of war back to Singapore where he experienced the brutality of his enemy. Gordon survived and eventually returned to Scotland and wrote a memoir of his experiences: *To End All Wars*.

In the horror of being a prisoner of war, Gordon saw and experienced the worst of humanity. From the beatings and hardships imposed by their captors, to the disease and a total loss of morale. In his memoir, he tells of how each man had to learn to live the "law of the jungle." It's what Tennyson called "red in tooth and claw"—it was the survival of the fittest. But things began to change for Gordon.

He tells the story of an unnamed man who worked as a prisoner on the railway. After the work had been done for the day, a Japanese guard said a shovel was missing. He lined all the prisoners up and in a fit of rage began asking who had stolen the shovel. Gordon says that the guard worked himself into a "paranoid fury," and when no one admitted stealing the shovel, he began to shriek: "All die! All die!" At that moment, the unnamed man stepped forward and calmly admitted, "I did it." The guard proceeded to beat him to death with his fists and the barrel of his gun. When the tools were all counted again, it was discovered that none were missing. One man had chosen to die for all. Movingly, Gordon wrote the following:

> It was dawning on us all—officers and other ranks alike—that the law of the jungle is not the law for man. We had seen for ourselves how quickly it could strip most of us of our humanity and reduce us to levels lower than beasts. . . . Death was still with us—no doubt about that. But we were slowly being freed from its destructive grip. We were seeing for ourselves the sharp contrast between the

> forces that made for life and those that made for death. Selfishness, hatred, envy, jealousy, greed, self-indulgence, laziness and pride were all anti-life. Love, heroism, self-sacrifice, sympathy, mercy, integrity and creative faith, on the other hand, were the essence of life, turning mere existence into living in its truest sense. These were gifts of God to men.

In the mud and the blood of his imprisonment, Gordon discovered the "more excellent way." He found the way of love and by faith traced it to the source of it all—the God who is love.

NOTHING WITHOUT LOVE

Yes, love is the most excellent way. Whether you were in ancient Corinth, shackled in a prison camp, or living the humdrum routines of modern life, *love is the best of all ways.* The apostle Paul illustrates this graphically. He wrote, "If I speak in the tongues of men and angels, but have not love, I am a noisy gong or a clanging cymbal" (1 Cor. 13:1). Of course, the "tongues of men" is a spiritual gift referred to previously in his letter, but Paul's point is far-reaching.

There are those who have a way with words. Think of Teddy Roosevelt's famous "The Man in the Arena" speech—the most widely quoted speech of his career. Or think of the way George S. Patton rallied the Third Army before their invasion of France in 1944. Words are powerful. They can command and motivate; they can win and influence; they can shape and form. But here's Paul's point. No matter how great and excellent your words are, if you don't have love, if love isn't behind the words, what is spoken is as useless as the resounding *clang, clang, clang* of a cymbal. It's why the apostle John said: "Little children, let us not love in word or talk but in deed and in truth" (1 John 3:18).

Paul went on to write, "And if I have prophetic powers, and understand all mysteries and knowledge, and if I have all faith, so as to remove mountains, but have not love, I am nothing" (1 Cor. 13:2). Again, he's using the spiritual gifts he's mentioned earlier. Why? Because spiritual gifts are the greatest personal gift the Spirit gives to a believer. His point is simple, but it's cutting. You can be the *most* spiritually gifted person in all the world, but if you don't possess love, you're nothing.

If that's true of spiritual gifts then it's also true of lesser gifts from God. James says, "Every good gift and every perfect gift is from above, coming down from the Father of lights" (James 1:17). Maybe you've been given a lot: a family, a roof over your head, money in your bank account, physical health, etc. Perhaps you want even more. The latest technology, a boat or camper, a loaded 401(k), a vacation home, a college degree, or whatever else we fill our lives with. Maybe you dream about the wealth, freedom, and security of men like Elon Musk and Jeff Bezos. But here's Paul's point: you could have all the world and its resources at your fingertips, but if you don't have love *you are nothing*.

Did you hear that? Paul goes as far to say that if he doesn't have love then he's nothing, he's a nobody—he's a zero. I know that's not the kind of message people want to be motivated by. Can you imagine if a motivational speaker tried to make a living by telling people, "Hey, you're a nobody"? That motivational speaker wouldn't have a job very long. However, that's what the Bible says. Not like some playground bully who is out to be a jerk. But Paul is calling a spade a spade. Without love, it doesn't matter what you have or possess.

As if that isn't enough, Paul went even further: "If I give away all I have, and if I deliver up my body to be burned, but have not love, I gain nothing" (1 Cor. 13:3). Now the emphasis shifts from *having* to *giving*. Clearly, the idea he's using here is giving to the poor. The first time I ever saw a homeless person was when my parents took us to Seattle. Right there on the sidewalk were people without possessions begging for money. Every now and then someone would throw a coin or crumpled bill into their cup, but most tried to avoid eye contact. Imagine, though, if the wealthiest person walked by and emptied his life savings into that cup. Paul says if he gives it without love, he's gained nothing. Then Paul ups the ante. He adds, "If I deliver up my body to be burned." He moves from giving what we have to giving our very selves—self-sacrifice in the most painful way imaginable. Even in our culture, we celebrate as heroic those who give their lives for others. It's the greatest possible sacrifice we can imagine, but if it's done without love, then nothing is gained.

Do you get Paul's point? He's painting the picture of an ideal man: great abilities, immensely successful, and tremendously generous. That's a man who can win friends and influence people. But what's the problem? If he doesn't have love, then it's all meaningless. It would be hard for him to find a stronger (and perhaps more manly) way of making his point. This brilliant and battered man is saying, "Love is the more excellent way." He digs his heels in. Nothing you *say*, nothing you *have*, and nothing you *give* matters in the slightest if you don't have love. It is love—not ability, success, or sacrifice—that makes or breaks a man. Love is that excellent. It's the most excellent thing.

5

THE PRIORITY OF LOVE

HERE'S THE PROBLEM: there's a runaway train speeding down the track. Ahead, on the tracks, are five people tied up and unable to move. The train is barreling straight for them. You are standing next to a lever that could switch the train to a different set of tracks. However, you notice that on the other tracks there is one person who is also tied up and unable to move. Now you have a choice. If you do nothing, the train will kill five people on the first track. If you pull the lever, switching the train to a different track, it will kill one person. *What's the right thing to do?*

I know it's an overused thought experiment—fun to think about on a boring car ride, though it has little use in everyday life. But the point is to create a dilemma for which there is not an obvious answer. It's also the kind of problem that the Pharisees enjoyed throwing at Jesus.

A DILEMMA

The Pharisees were a group of religious leaders in the New Testament. They knew their Old Testament really well—they probably had most of it memorized. They were also experts in Jewish tradition and law. One of them once cornered Jesus and asked him, "Teacher, which is the great commandment in the Law?" (Matt. 22:36). It may seem to be a silly question, but it was supposed to put Jesus in a dilemma. In the teachings of the Rabbis, there were more than 600 commands. Jesus was the son of a carpenter whose best friends were blue-collar fishermen. These guys basically had PhDs in "Jewish Law," and they wanted an answer.

Let me pause and try to get you to relate to the dilemma. Pretend someone asks you, "What's the most important law when you've driving?" Actually, let me make it a little easier. Let's ask, "Is it more important to stop at a stop sign or go the speed limit?" How would you answer? I'd guess most of us would say it's probably more important to stop at a stop sign. Oh, but wait a minute! If you say that, does it mean it's better to speed through a school zone where kids are present? Obviously not. We can't endanger children. So then, is it better to run a stop sign where you might hit someone?

On and on it goes. And that's only two laws. How was Jesus supposed to pick from more than 600?

However, Jesus was always one step ahead of the bullies. The Pharisees wanted to argue about rituals, cleansing, circumcision, and sacrifices. But Jesus said, "You shall love the Lord your God with all your heart and with all your soul and with all your mind. This is the great and first commandment. And a second is like it: You shall love your neighbor as yourself" (Matt. 22:37–39). There it is! See what Jesus did? He turned the tables. Jesus says it's *love.* He puts the priority on love. I bet the Pharisees weren't expecting that!

THE ORDER OF LOVE

While love is the priority, Jesus's answer isn't simply, "You need to love." He also says there are two directions to love. The first is love in the vertical direction—*love to God.* The second is love in the horizontal direction—*love to neighbor.* This is really important. If we're going to hear the voice of God in the Bible about what Christianity says love is, we need to pay careful attention. There's an order to the love that Jesus speaks about.

Jesus doesn't say that the great commandment is to love God and neighbor as though it was a single command. He also doesn't say the great command is to love your neighbor and the second is to love God. No. There's a purposeful ordering in the priority of love. The great command is to love God, and the second command is to love your neighbor. But love for a neighbor is always second to the love of God.

Why is that important? Today we hear a lot about the need to love. In one sense, everyone seems to recognize the universal appeal of it—songwriters, cultural influencers, Hollywood actors, psychologists, politicians, and philosophers. Maybe you know the lyrics to this Lenny Kravitz song: "It's time to take a stand; brothers and sisters join hands, we got to let love rule." People say it's all we need, and it's the one thing there's just too little of. Putting definitions aside about what that "love" means, the bigger problem is that the focus is entirely on the horizontal direction—love to neighbor. *This is not the priority of the Bible.* Love to God is the first and great commandment and love to neighbor is the second.

THE GREAT COMMANDMENT

One of the first times I spoke at a funeral, I did my best to tell people that the only confident way to meet death is through faith in Jesus Christ. Afterward, a man came up to me to thank me for my message. He said I hit the nail on the head. He went on to say, "You said the right thing. All that matters in this life is that we believe. It doesn't matter *who* or *what* we believe in, it just matters that we believe." I was shocked. That wasn't my message! Was this a passive-aggressive attempt to actually undercut what I said, or was this man that tone deaf?

It might be easy to hear Jesus's words with a similar inattention. But we can't make Jesus say something other than what he said. When he names the first and greatest commandment as loving *God*, he doesn't mean you need to love *your* god—whoever or whatever that might be. This isn't a command to love Allah, Shiva, Brahma, Buddha, Vishnu, or your favorite sports team. There is only one true and living God—the God of the Bible—Father, Son, and Holy Spirit—the God who is love. Jesus is saying the greatest command is to love the one God. Allah is not God. Buddha is not a god. All the religions of this world don't teach what Jesus says here.

How is God to be loved? Jesus says: "You shall love the Lord your God with all your heart and with all your soul and with all your mind." Heart. Soul. Mind. Strength. We don't need to overanalyze this. It's a forceful way to make a simple point. It's a way of saying that the greatest commandment is to love God with everything you are. That's how you're to love God. Nothing is excluded. We are commanded to love God with our attitude. We're commanded to love him with our intelligence. We're to love him with our emotions. We're to love him with our reason, resources, motives, plans, and will. It's not enough to love God half-heartedly. It's not enough to love him quarter-heartedly. It's not enough to love God in 99 percent of who I am. He needs to be loved wholly. All the life and power within me is to be given in loving God.

THE SECOND COMMANDMENT

Next, there is also a horizontal direction of love: "You shall love your neighbor as yourself." Obviously, the big question is "Who is my neighbor?" That's the question a hot-shot lawyer asked Jesus (Luke 10:29). When we think of a neighbor, we think of those who live next to us—whether it's right next door or, if you live out in the country, the person a couple miles down the road. But Jesus isn't being restricted. He's not saying you need to simply love the old woman who lives on the other side of the fence. Rather, he's throwing the door wide open. Who is my neighbor? Anyone you come into contact with. Everyone you come into contact with.

That's how broad love is to extend. Jesus isn't saying, "The second command is to love those who are easy to love." He's not saying I need to love only those people who believe like I do or look like me or act like me or talk like me. Jesus isn't saying we need to love a certain social class—the rich but not the poor, or the poor but not the rich. Jesus isn't saying we get to pick and choose people from a certain ethnicity or those with a certain skin color. Jesus doesn't limit this love to those people who aren't annoying, don't have personality quirks that get under our skin, or who don't inconvenience us. Jesus isn't even saying we need to love only our spouse, children, or grandchildren. No. Our neighbor is everyone and anyone brought into the sphere of personal contact.

Then Jesus really hammers the nail in: we are to love God with all of our heart, soul, and mind. How are you to love your neighbor? *As yourself.* It would be easy to get bogged down in details. Yes, there is a self-love that makes us selfish, like that two-year-old who throws a temper tantrum because he didn't get what he wants, or the full-grown man who . . . also throws a more sophisticated temper tantrum for the same reason. But if we keep our eye on the ball, it's a simple point. Jesus takes for granted that there is a self-love that is the measure of our love to neighbor. There's a self-interest that motivates us to do things. And Jesus is saying the same way you're interested in yourself—your needs, wants, concerns—you need to do that for your neighbor.

Jesus is faced with a dilemma. But rather than bounce back and forth between multiple options, he walks around the question to get to its heart. What is the greatest commandment? The greatest commandment is to love God and the second—and yes, it's second in order—is to love your neighbor as yourself.

6
THE RULE OF LOVE

I GREW UP IN THE BEST NEIGHBORHOOD. We lived off the road from one of the busiest streets in our town, so we didn't get a lot of useless traffic. There was a public playground at the end of the cul-de-sac, and beyond that, open cornfields. Even in our small rural community in south-central Minnesota, our "block" (as we called it) probably had two dozen kids my age. Summer days would find us outside from sunup until well past sundown, riding bikes, playing cops and robbers, or our crazy and fun "night games."

My parents and the parents of the neighborhood hardly had to keep an eye on us. While we enjoyed the sense of freedom no matter where we went and what we did, my parents' rules always seemed to follow. Before crossing the street, I had to look both ways. I wasn't allowed to play in the ravine adjacent to the neighborhood or wander into the cornfield when the stalks were higher than my head. If we went to the nearby lake to swim, we had to let them know. And, don't ask for details, but we were absolutely forbidden from climbing on the neighbor's roof or throwing rocks at passing cars.

Like all kids, the rules sometimes felt like a killjoy to me. When I was feeling snarly, I'd challenge my parents. "Why can't I run around in the cornfield at night?" Of course, there are all kinds of good reasons to not do that. It's easy to become lost in a cornfield when you can't see over it. There are potential hazards, and if you get hurt, it would be hard to find you. Or trampling through a cornfield could ruin part of a farmer's hard-earned harvest. But sometimes it's hard to reason with a ten-year-old, so often they simply replied, "Because we love you."

GIVEN IN LOVE

Whatever childish logic tells us, rules aren't in opposition to love. Because I love my five kids, I tell them they cannot run into the busy street in front of our house. We had a cat that did that once . . . and he only did it once. So it shouldn't surprise us that the God who is love has also given us rules. When God first spoke the Ten Commandments, before he got to the commands, he said: "I am the LORD your God, who brought you out of the land of Egypt, out of the house of slavery" (Exod. 20:2). It was because of God's love that he rescued his people from Egypt, and it's also by that love that he gave them the rules they needed to live by.

Fast forward a couple thousand years. The night before he was crucified, Jesus ate a final meal with his disciples. The dinner table conversation wasn't small talk or chitchat. Rather, after three years with his disciples, Jesus saved some of his most important teaching for this night. On that evening he told them, "This is my commandment, that you love one another as I have loved you" (John 14:12). While it's the last thing he mentioned in the sentence, his love for them is first. Love others *as I have loved you*. Even this command was given to the disciples as part of the way in which Jesus gave his love to them.

We need to remember this because it's easy to let childish logic take over. Here's what I mean: we sometimes associate love with autonomy. Whoa, what does that mean? *Autonomy* is a word that means having control over yourself. I remember an ex-girlfriend breaking up with me said, "If you love me, you'll let me go. Just let me do what I want." Now, I won't argue if she was right or wrong, but I bring up that example to say we sometimes treat God that way. Here's what it sounds like: "Because he's a God of love, he doesn't care what my sexuality is—straight, gay, or bisexual," or "Because he's a God of love, he understands why I'm getting a divorce from my wife," or "Because he's a God of love he wants me to pursue my dreams." It all goes back to the assumption that love promotes autonomy. But that isn't true. God's love doesn't give us autonomy, it gives us rules and boundaries in which to live.

GIVING LOVE

Not only are God's rules given as an act of love, but they guide us on how to give love. In the last chapter, we focused on Jesus's teaching: "You shall love the Lord your God with all your heart and with all your soul and with all your mind. This is the great and first commandment. And a second is like it: You shall love your neighbor as yourself" (Matt. 22:37–39). We saw that love is the priority, that love has an order, and that love has two directions. But *how* do we love God and neighbor?

We love God and neighbor by the rules that God has given us. Jesus said, "If you love me, you will keep my commandments" (John 14:15). Paul wrote, "The one who loves another has fulfilled the law" (Rom. 13:8). John wrote, "For this is the love of God, that we keep his commandments. And his commandments are not burdensome" (1 John 5:3), and later he said, "And this is love, that we walk according to his commandments" (2 John 6).

Does this surprise you? It shouldn't. Let me give you a couple of examples. First, let's pick the low-hanging fruit.

A married man doesn't get to go have sex with a woman who isn't his wife and then tell his wife: "I committed adultery *because I love you.*" That would be ludicrous! Adultery, which God forbids in his law, *cannot* and *is not* an expression of love. You can't love another person while committing adultery. Or, as another example, kids cannot at the same time love their parents while disobeying them. If I say to my son, "Take the garbage out," and he says, "No thanks because I love you," something doesn't add up! Disobedience is not an expression of love. That's because love finds its concrete expression not apart from the rules of God, but through the rules he has given.

TEN RULES OF LOVE

What are those rules? Jesus said that the first and second commandments hung on the law of God (see Matt. 22:40). In the Bible, the best summary of God's law is found in the Ten Commandments. If you break the commandments up, you might realize that there are two parts. The first four commandments have to do with loving God and the last six with loving our neighbor.

The first in the Ten Commandments is, "You shall have no other gods before me" (Exod. 20:3). God is saying that there is no other god except him, Father, Son, and Holy Spirit. Islam's Allah is not a god. Buddah is not a god. The Hindu gods are no gods at all! God is also saying no one and nothing can come before him. To love God means you take him to be your God and you prioritize him above everything—yourself, your family, money, comfort, pleasure, fun, and so on.

The second command about carving images and bowing down to them (Exod. 20:4–6) tells us that we love God by worshiping him as he wants to be worshiped. A lot of Christians may not think much about this. But God cares *how* we worship, and he tells us in the Bible how we should do that. To worship him as he has commanded is a way we love him.

The third command says, "You shall not take the name of the LORD your God in vain" (Exod. 20:7). Simply put, we are to love God by recognizing who he is and responding to him in a way that is appropriate to who he is. For instance, using his name as an expletive or exclamation—as so many people do—is *not* respecting who he is, and it's not loving him.

The fourth commandment about remembering the Sabbath and keeping it holy (see Exod. 20:8–11) tells us that we're to love God by setting aside time each week—actually a whole day—to focus on and rest in him.

The last six commands of the Ten Commandments teach us how we should love each other. An old writer named Ezekiel Hopkins summarized these six commands as showing love to our neighbor's honor, physical selves, wealth and possessions, and reputation.

The fifth commandment is about honoring your father and mother (Exod. 20:12) and tells us to love others by giving them what they deserve: "Pay to all what is owed to them. . . . respect to whom respect is owed, honor to whom honor is owed" (Rom. 13:7).

The sixth commandment says, "You shall not murder" (Exod. 20:13). We love others through preserving and protecting their lives.

The seventh commandment is "You shall not commit adultery" (Exod. 20:14). Any and all sexual activity and experiences outside of a biblically defined marriage—a marriage between one man and one woman in a lifelong commitment—isn't an expression of love.

The eighth commandment says, "You shall not steal," the ninth commandment is "You shall not bear false witness," and the tenth commandment says, "You shall not covet" (Exod. 20:15–17)—we love others by not taking what isn't ours, by being truthful in all things, and by not being envious of the things they have.

Of course, that's the 20,000-foot flyover of the commands. Each of them can be expanded and applied in all kinds of ways. The point, however, is simply this: God's rules tell us how we are to love him and love others. Thoughts, words, and actions that go against those rules aren't loving God or our neighbor. To disobey them isn't to express love, but to hurt and wrong another.

Think about that. A man who spends his Sundays for himself—sleeping in, watching football, drinking beer, going fishing—isn't loving God. A child who dishonors her mom and dad isn't loving her parents. A young man who has premarital sex with his girlfriend isn't actually loving her. As Paul wrote, "For the commandments, 'You shall not commit adultery, You shall not murder, You shall not steal, You shall not covet,' and any other commandment, are summed up in this word: 'You shall love your neighbor as yourself.' Love does no wrong to a neighbor; therefore love is the fulfilling of the law" (Rom. 13:9–10).

The God who is love gives us these rules so we can love him and others, which is the most excellent way.

7
LOVE LOST, LOVE FOUND

DURING MY HIGH SCHOOL YEARS, I worked at a summer camp in northern Minnesota. A favorite game of staff and campers alike was "Flashlight Wars." The whole camp was divided into eight teams—each consisting of forty to fifty people. Cones were hidden in the woods, and under the cover of darkness, two team captains were to lead the whole group silently through the woods, snag a cone, and return to base to declare victory. The only weapons were our flashlights, and if a team happened upon the enemy, they would give a burst of light and send them back to start.

Of course, other teams weren't the only opponent. The darkness was one too. When I said "under the cover of darkness," we're talking really dark. It was, after all, northern

Minnesota. Away from the city and its lights and under the canopy of trees, we were hardly able to see our hands in front of our faces. That meant when I got the chance to be a captain, I had to go in broad daylight and scope out the path, making one—or many—mental maps of where and how to guide my team. It was easy in the light. However, it was almost impossible in the dark. Though I thought I knew the way, I and the other team captain got hopelessly turned around and lost in the middle of the woods. Finally, we gave up, turned our flashlights on, and with the help of the light wandered back to the main camp. The darkness had won.

A WORLD OF LOVE

It's always been a little funny to me that the Bible doesn't start with a defense of the existence of God. Nope. It doesn't. In fact, the Bible never defends his existence. It takes it for granted and asserts its truth. Thus, the Bible opens with those words: "In the beginning, God created the heavens and the earth" (Gen. 1:1).

In that original creation—as the God who is love divided light and dark; made the earth, sea, and sky; filled his creation with vegetation and animals; and created man—everything was as it should be. We read, "And God saw everything that he had made, and behold, it was very good" (Gen. 1:31).

This goodness extended to the relationship God had with the first man and first woman, Adam and Eve. In fact, we read that God planted a garden and then placed Adam in it, and afterward in that garden God created Eve. The garden was a place of fellowship for God and man. We read that God would walk in the garden during the cool of the day (Gen. 3:8). It was a place where God loved Adam and Eve, and where they with heart, soul, and mind loved him in return.

It was also a place of neighborly love. God had seen that Adam was alone, and so he made Eve. Drawn by desire, Adam was quite taken with her, and they united together as man and wife. He was bound to her with a loving affection, and she was his loving companion. In the bonds of love we read that they "were both naked and were not ashamed" (Gen. 2:25).

An old Scottish writer named Hugh Binning said in his *Treatise of Christian Love*:

> As God molded the rest of the world into a beautiful frame, by the first stamp of his finger, so he did engrave upon the hearts of men such a principle, as might be a perpetual bond and tie to unite the sons of men together. This was nothing else but the law of love, the principal fundamental law of our creation, love to God, founded on that essential dependence and subordination to God, and love to man, grounded upon that communion and interest in one image of God.

The God who is love had created a world he loved and one who loved him, and he put his creation into a loving relationship with each other.

LOVE LOST

Tragically, as we read the history of humanity in the opening chapters of Genesis, that world of love was lost. God had given to Adam a rule of love: "And the Lord God commanded the man, saying, 'You may surely eat of every tree of the garden, but of the tree of the knowledge of good and evil you shall not eat'" (Gen. 2:16–17). That rule would prove the test of Adam's love—would he obey the God of love or not? But, as you may well know the history, Adam and Eve chose to reject the rule of love, and in so doing, they rejected the love of God by eating of the tree. In that one decisive act, they shattered the loving relationship between God and man. Rather than live in mutual love and fellowship with him, they hid from his presence (Gen. 3:8). The love Adam had for God was lost.

This selfish act, however, not only broke the relationship of love between them and God, it also broke their loving relationship with one another. When God asks Adam if he ate from the tree, what does Adam do? He says, "The woman whom you gave to be with me, she gave me fruit of the tree, and I ate" (Gen. 3:12). Far from an innocent retelling of the facts, Adam is dodging responsibility. He throws his wife under the bus. A husband who does that isn't honorable and manly. He's a coward. What a sad turn of events. Adam began by saying, "Bone of my bones and flesh of my flesh" (Gen. 2:23) and comes now to say, "The woman whom you gave to be with me" (Gen. 3:12). Lost is the love he shared with Eve.

That is what happened when Adam and Eve sinned. The vertical and horizontal relationships of love were ruined—not only for them but for all who are born from them. Sin has cast a cloud of the deepest darkness over a world of love, and we've entirely lost our way. In the place of love is hatred, enmity, division, contempt, and bitterness. That's not true of just a couple people here and there or a few people to the exclusion of the rest. No. This is our default. As those born in sin and under the power of sin, we've lost love.

This is how Paul characterizes us: "haters of God" (Rom. 1:30) and "hostile to God" (Rom. 8:7). It's why John says, "Not that we have loved God" (1 John 4:10). It's why Jesus said, "Whoever hates me hates my Father also" (John 15:23). The Bible tells us in no uncertain or unclear terms that by nature, we are born at odds with God. Sure, you may not be hostile toward him like Richard Dawkins, a British biologist and author. I forget where, but I once read that Dawkins had chosen to make God his number one enemy. But you're not like that. No, you may not be antagonistic or hostile, but remember the command. The command is to love God with *all* your heart, mind, and strength. I assure you, you don't do that.

Being cut off from God who is love—the source of all true love—you also hate your neighbor. "Wait a second!" you might protest. "Do I really hate my neighbor? After all, I'm a pretty good guy. I love my wife and children, I try to do good by other people. How can you say I hate my neighbor?" Well, what happens when you unplug an electrical device? Of course, it no longer works. The power has been cut off. A ruined relationship with God leads to a ruined relationship with others. Still unsure? Okay, hear me out.

Jesus said, "You have heard that it was said to those of old, 'You shall not murder; and whoever murders will be liable to judgment.' But I say to you that everyone who is angry with his brother will be liable to judgment" (Matt. 5:21–22). What is Jesus doing? He's going deeper into the command. Suppose someone heard Jesus say, "You shall not murder." We might be led to say, "Great! I've never killed anyone. I'm good to go!" Ah, but here's Jesus's point. The command goes further than a physical killing. If you've been angry, Jesus is saying you're guilty of murder.

Or, consider what Paul wrote: "Let love be genuine" (Rom. 12:9). The word *genuine* means "without hypocrisy." What's hypocrisy? When I was a boy, my mom would sometimes take me to the local donut shop. On the front counter was a plate of donuts that was picture perfect. Being the kind of guy who especially likes frosting, I extended my finger to swipe a little from the donut on the counter one morning. Much to my surprise, my finger hit only hard plastic. Believe me, to a six-year-old, that donut looked real! But it wasn't. That's hypocrisy—to have the appearance of something but not the truth of it. Paul says that love can't have the slightest insincerity. Have you always loved your wife, your children, or that obnoxious person at work with a genuine love? I didn't think so.

LOVE FOUND

Here we are. Wandering in a world of darkness. Fellowship with the God who is love has been lost, and we've been plunged into a world of hatred, animosity, and bitterness. When I turn on the news channel and see the daily reports of crime and murder, or watch the political parties snarl and fight each other, or watch as social media brings out the best . . . err, I mean the worst of us, or when I look into my own heart through the lens of the first and second commandments, it often seems that the darkness has won. But the main storyline of the Bible is that the darkness—hatred—hasn't won.

> For God so loved the world, that he gave his only Son, that whoever believes in him should not perish but have eternal life. For God did not send his

Son into the world to condemn the world, but in order that the world might be saved through him. Whoever believes in him is not condemned, but whoever does not believe is condemned already, because he has not believed in the name of the only Son of God. (John 3:16–18)

For while we were still weak, at the right time Christ died for the ungodly. For one will scarcely die for a righteous person—though perhaps for a good person one would dare even to die—but God shows his love for us in that while we were still sinners, Christ died for us. (Rom. 5:6–8)

But God, being rich in mercy, because of the great love with which he loved us, even when we were dead in our trespasses, made us alive together with Christ—by grace you have been saved—and raised us up with him and seated us with him in the heavenly places in Christ Jesus, so that in the coming ages he might show the immeasurable riches of his grace in kindness toward us in Christ Jesus. (Eph. 2:4–7)

In this the love of God was made manifest among us, that God sent his only Son into the world, so that we might live through him. In this is love, not that we have loved God but that he loved us and sent his Son to be the propitiation for our sins. (1 John 4:9–10)

There are many different ways to express it, but all say the same thing. The God of love, out of the overflowing abundance of his love, has sent his only-begotten and greatly loved Son that we might be saved through faith in the knowledge of Jesus Christ. And as we come to know him, he restores that which has been lost in sin—a loving relationship with God and with one another. You see, this is why not believing in Jesus is so serious. It's rejecting the love of God. But to believe is to come to be oriented around his love. Again, John writes,

> And by this we know that we have come to know him, if we keep his commandments. Whoever says "I know him" but does not keep his commandments is a liar, and the truth is not in him, but whoever keeps his word, in him truly the love of God is perfected. (1 John 2:3–5)

8

RELATIONSHIPS OF LOVE

SOMETIMES MY WIFE AND I like to play a game with our kids. We ask them to decide which parent they love more.

Now that I actually write this out it seems almost like a cruel form of torture, but it's all in good fun. In case you care, Mom usually wins. Now and then one of them will retaliate and ask me: "Who do you love more: me or Mom?" But, ever prepared for their challenge, I have a ready answer.

That's because my love for my daughter is a different kind of love than the love I have for my wife. So I can tell her when she asks: "It's not about who I love more because I don't love you the same." I win!

DIFFERENT LOVE

The ancient Greeks distinguished between different kinds of love. In broad and sweeping strokes, they mostly talked about four: *eros, storge, philia,* and *agape*. Why did they need four words? It's for the reason I mentioned above. It's because we love different people in different ways. Who that person is to us and the nature of our relationship determines the appropriate way we are to express love.

At the risk of being extremely simplistic, the way the Greeks defined the four types of love would be these: *Eros* (think here of "erotic") is a love of passion or what we might commonly call romantic love. *Storge* is a love of natural affection like a child has for a parent or a parent for a child. *Philia* is a love of delight the way we enjoy the company of a friend. In fact, the city of Philadelphia is nicknamed "The City of Brotherly Love," as its name is the combination of this kind of love and the word for brother. Then there is *agape*. This is a cherishing or prizing kind of love. To quote a really smart guy named Benjamin Warfield (and to make the Greek he uses readable): "If we should endeavor to hit off the special implication of each with a single word, we might perhaps say that with *storge* is nature, with *eros* passion, *philia* pleasurableness, and with *agape* preciousness."

Times change and so too does the use of language. Just look at what the teenagers text each other and try to decipher what they're saying. It's gobbledygook. In our everyday English, we don't use these old words. I don't tell my kids, "I *storge* you" or my wife, "I *eros* you." We just use "love." But there are different relationships for love. To impress you, let me quote another smart guy named Jonathan Edwards:

> All true Christian love is one and the same in its principle. It may be various in its forms and objects, and may be exercised either toward God or men, but it is the same principle in the heart that is the foundation of every exercise of a truly Christian love, whatever may be its object. (*Love, the Sum of All Virtue*)

GOD AND PEOPLE

Maybe it's a tad jarring, but God doesn't love people in the same way. What? Is that even possible? There is a love that God has for all and it expresses itself in daily kindness—we might even call it his goodwill. Jesus taught:

> But I say to you, Love your enemies and pray for those who persecute you, so that you may be sons of your Father who is in heaven. For he makes the sun to rise on the evil and on the good, and sends rain on the just and on the unjust. (Matt. 5:44–45)

Did you catch that? Why should followers of Jesus love their enemies? Because their Father loves his enemies: the evil and unjust.

But God has more than goodwill for his own people. That shouldn't surprise us. After all, those who believe in Jesus are adopted into God's family and have God as their Father (1 John 3:1). No dad loves the kid down the street in the same way he loves his own son. Jesus said, "And he who loves me will be loved by my Father, and I will love him and manifest myself to him" (John 14:21). Another picture of the special relationship between God and his people is that of a husband and bride. We read, "I will betroth you to me forever" (Hos. 2:19). In the New Testament, that's the image of the relationship between Jesus and the church. No husband loves every woman the way he loves his wife. It's a special love.

PARENTS AND CHILDREN

One of the closest and strongest love relationships is between parents and children. That's why God likens his love for us in this way—telling us not only of his love but what it means to love as a parent. We read, "As a father shows compassion to his children, so the LORD shows compassion to those who fear him" (Ps. 103:13). We're also told, "For the Lord disciplines the one he loves, and he chastises every son whom he receives" (Heb. 12:6).

God doesn't even shy away from using motherly pictures—even though God is always a "he" and never a "she" and "Father" not "Mother" and we shouldn't call him such. God asks, "Can a woman forget her nursing child, that she should have no compassion on the son of her womb? Even these may forget, yet I will not forget you" (Isa. 49:15). And Jesus says, "How often would I have gathered your children together as a hen gathers her brood under her wings" (Luke 13:34). We could add other things. Mothers are to be gentle and affectionate, and fathers should encourage and charge their children to walk with God (1 Thess. 2:7–8, 11–12).

Likewise, children love their parents. As they do so, they're called to obey and honor their dad and mom (Eph. 6:1), listen to their words of wisdom and godly counsel (Prov. 1:8), receive discipline from them (Heb. 12:9), and even care for them in old age (1 Tim. 5:4).

HUSBAND AND WIFE

Marriage is another relationship of love. The biblical definition of marriage is between one man and one woman (Matt. 19:5). It's a relationship where mother and father are left in order for husband and wife to be one (Gen. 2:24). Marriage is intended for good and for mutual delight (Prov. 5:18–19), for physical and sexual intimacy (1 Cor. 7:3–5), and both husband and wife are to keep the marriage bed pure (Heb. 13:4). This relationship is wound so tightly that there are only a couple reasons for which the Bible permits divorce (Matt. 19:9 and 1 Cor. 7:15).

Wives are called to love their husbands and be submissive to them (Titus 2:4–5) even if they aren't Christians (1 Peter 3:1). Likewise, husbands are to love their wives with self-sacrifice and to cherish them (Eph. 5:25, 29). Husbands are to love their wives in an understanding way as someone who is weaker (1 Peter 3:7).

FELLOW CHRISTIANS

When Jesus was preparing to go to the cross, he taught his disciples an important lesson. He said, "A new commandment I give to you, that you love one another: just as I have loved you, you also are to love one another. By this all people will know that you are my disciples, if you have love for one another" (John 13:34–35). The relationship that we have with fellow Christians—our brothers and sisters in Jesus—is a relationship of love.

This is so important. Paul says we should "Love one another with brotherly affection" (Rom. 12:10). He goes on to say that love is a debt we owe to others that can never be repaid (Rom. 13:8). Peter emphasized this particular love, too, when he wrote, "Honor everyone. Love the brotherhood" (1 Peter 2:17). In fact, it's so important to love other believers that John says, "If anyone says, 'I love God,' and hates his brother, he is a liar" (1 John 4:20).

FRIENDSHIP

Friendship is an important theme in the Bible. We're warned that it matters who our friends are because "Bad company ruins good morals" (1 Cor. 15:33). A good friend, however, is of great value: "A man of many companions may come to ruin, but there is a friend who sticks closer than a brother" (Prov. 18:24). This relationship is also a relationship of love: "A friend loves at all times" (Prov. 17:17).

It's hard to think of friendship and the Bible without thinking of one of the closest friendships in the Bible. One of the most celebrated biblical characters is David. He was a shepherd who fought on the battlefield against the giant Goliath and took his head off. From there, David became a man of war. The women used to dance and sing, "Saul has struck down his thousands, and David his ten thousands" (1 Sam. 18:7). He was also a songwriter and became known as "the sweet psalmist of Israel" (2 Sam. 23:1). Later he would become king of Israel, and his wealth and fame knew no end. David was the real deal. A man's man of great renown.

This shepherd-turned-warrior-turned-king was also known for his friendship with Jonathan: "The soul of Jonathan was knit to the soul of David, and Jonathan loved him as his own soul" (1 Sam. 18:1). When Jonathan died, David wept and cried, "I am distressed for you, my brother Jonathan; very pleasant have you been to me; your love to me was extraordinary, surpassing the love of women" (2 Sam. 1:26).

In our hyper-sexualized culture, that language may be awkward. But it's not some kind of homoerotic expression—David and Jonathan were not gay. Rather, it's a deep expression of the love of a friend that is unlike any other love in this world. Men who have served in conflicts and war together can probably relate with the sense of brotherhood David expresses. No wonder Jesus tells his disciples: "No longer do I call you servants. . . . but I have called you friends" (John 15:15).

ENEMIES

God, parents, children, spouse, friends . . . those are life's very best relationships. When things are working like a well-oiled machine, they're also mutual. God loves us and we love God; children love parents and parents love children; husbands love their wives and wives love their husbands; friends love each other. There is, however, another relationship of love, and it doesn't fit this pattern. The Christian is to love even their enemy: "You have heard that it was said, 'You shall love your neighbor and hate your enemy.' But I say to you, Love your enemies" (Matt. 5:43–44).

That's right. Love those who only hate you in return. Love those who respond with evil. Love those who retaliate with harm and hurt. Christians are to love their enemies. Who can love like that? Only someone who has known the love of God first. That's because this is what his love has done. Paul says, "But God shows his love for us in that while we were still sinners, Christ died for us" (Rom. 5:8). What does it mean to be a "sinner"? The answer is a couple verses away: "For if while we were enemies we were reconciled to God by the death of his Son, much more, now that we are reconciled, shall we be saved by his life" (Rom. 5:10). To be a sinner is to be an enemy. The God of love loved us when we were enemies, and that same love—poured into our hearts by the Holy Spirit—creates in us the capacity to love our enemies.

We have so many different relationships in life, and the ones listed here are some of the most important. Those relationships involve different people, different commitments, and different feelings. But every single one of them—however different they are—is united in this one thing: *each is to be a relationship where love is given and expressed.* So, as we come to those chapters that talk about what love *is* and *isn't*, we should find that it's applicable to every significant relationship in our life—with God, our parents, children, spouse, friends, and even our enemies.

9

LOVE IS PATIENT AND KIND

LOVE IS THE MOST excellent way. Whether it's in our vertical relationship with God or our horizontal relationships with our neighbors, the way of love is the best way to follow.

As we've seen, the congregation in Corinth needed to be reminded of that. Often, we do too. A few years ago, I found a stack of old papers and binders tucked away in a giant safe in the corner of my tornado shelter. It sounds eerie, but it wasn't. As I flipped through the paperwork, I found that it was a history of the congregation I pastor in Kansas. I read about the good things, and I read about the bad things.

FORGETTING LOVE

Sixty years ago, the congregation went through a rough season. I don't know all that happened, but there were strong personalities and disagreements (two ingredients that often mix like fire and gas). It became a huge explosion. In a letter written to the congregation it was said, "This church has forgotten about love." How sad. A church that exists to worship the God who is love because of the love he showed in sending his beloved Son whose love is poured into hearts by the Holy Spirit had forgotten love.

It can happen. I don't think that's because most of us willingly forget love. It's not like we sit down and say: "Nope! No more. I'm done." Some people do, but that's not the way it always happens. Often, love is slowly forgotten. Selfishness starts sticking its elbows into love's space at the dinner table, or arrogance starts to encroach. I remember flying once from Los Angeles back to Kansas on a red-eye flight. I was seated next to a large man who bit by bit took over my seat until I suddenly realized that I was leaning hard left and hanging halfway into the aisle. Husbands and wives can forget to love. Parents and children can forget to love. Friends can forget to love. And it's easy to forget to love your enemies. This forgetfulness is what happened in Corinth. Instead of walking in love, they had grown envious, boastful, and self-focused. So, Paul picked up his pen to give them a bit of a written spanking. He picked up his pen to tell them love has to push back.

I'm glad he did! What we get in 1 Corinthians 13 is a chapter of the Bible that simply portrays for us what love *is* and what love *isn't*. Now, I know that this chapter is often read at weddings. That's fine. Weddings are a celebration of marital love. But maybe it's worth pointing out that it wasn't written for a wedding. It was written to help us understand love for *all* of our relationships in life. It helps us know what it means to love God, to love your husband or wife, to love your parents or children, to love other people in the church, to love your friends, and to love your enemies.

DEFENSE AND OFFENSE

The first thing Paul writes about love is that "Love is patient and kind" (1 Cor. 13:4). These two belong together. When I was in second grade, I found a new passion that would carry me through the next four years: Tae Kwon-Do. When I was just beginning, my instructor taught me that martial arts involves both a good defense and offense. If you're only reacting to your opponent you'll be at a disadvantage, and if you're only assaulting your opponent you're likely to get exploited. A well-trained student will be equally equipped for both.

Of course, this isn't only true of martial arts. A good defense and offense are necessary in a lot of things. It's true of almost every sport. It's also needed in times of war. It's a concept that is used in the workplace and business world.

Lawyers in courtrooms know their cases depend on both. Even trivial things like board games can be won or lost depending on your defense and offense.

I don't know if you've ever thought of love this way, but that's how patience and kindness work. To borrow from the world of sports or business or military, patience is love's defense and kindness is love's offense.

IS PATIENT

Generally, when we think of patience we think about someone's ability to not get upset. In fact, you probably have a patient person come to mind. For some, it was Grandma and Grandpa. After a lifetime of experience, they seem to never run dry on patience. For others, it's your mom. There are probably few people on planet earth who put up with more nonsense than mothers. And while sometimes they've "had it up to *here* with you," they can be one of the best pictures of patience. Or maybe it's a schoolteacher. I tried substituting once for a kindergarten class in our local school district. Needless to say, I don't think I'll be trying that again.

Biblically, patience is so much more than just not getting upset. Patience is really the simpler word we use for long-suffering. To be patient means you suffer long. That's a colorful way to think about it. Why? Because the word *patience* involves suffering. A basic dictionary definition of suffering might be: experiencing pain, distress, or hardship.

What is patience? Patience is long-suffering—suffering *long*.

If you know the Bible, you know that there's a man who is known for patience. It's Job. In the Old Testament, we read that Job suffered—probably more than any other man except Jesus Christ. Job's children died, his servants were killed, he lost all that he owned (and he was really rich!), and his body was bent over in pain and disease. What did he do? He suffered long. In the New Testament we read,

> As an example of suffering and patience, brothers, take the prophets who spoke in the name of the Lord. Behold, we consider those blessed who remained steadfast. You have heard of the steadfastness of Job, and you have seen the purpose of the Lord, how the Lord is compassionate and merciful. (James 5:10–11)

Job is a drastic example of patience, but let's put this idea into our everyday relationships. Those who are closest to us can cause us to suffer. Simply put, other people can be a pain in the butt. Husbands and wives can hurt the other with words and actions, parents can be overbearing and children insufferable, people in the church can be difficult, friendships can sometimes be hard, and enemies can cause immense suffering in our lives.

What is love? Love is patient. It suffers long. It resists the temptation to return hardship with hardship; to render suffering for suffering. It doesn't give knee-jerk reactions or shoot from the hip. If you're married, you know what it's like to get into an argument with your husband or wife. Something hurtful is said or done, and it's easy—really easy—to return fire in the moment. That's not what love does. It's patient.

That doesn't mean that love makes us a doormat or that you're supposed to be walked all over. Love recognizes suffering. It's able to admit it and call it what it is. It is hardship, it is pain, and it does hurt. But patience is an active defense. Just because a battle-weary soldier knew that a volley of arrows was about to rain down on him didn't mean he should spread his arms wide and take one to the chest. No, heavy and tired as his arms are in the heat of the fight, he grabbed his shield and held it high. That takes strength. Rolling over and playing dead doesn't.

Patience isn't surrender. Patience is absorbing the blow of suffering. It's absorbing the anger and bitterness, the contempt or unfairness, the deceit and slander, the gossip or cruelty that's hurled at you. Sometimes patience does that by overlooking and covering a sin: "Love covers a multitude of sins" (1 Peter 4:8), and other times—when that's hard or nearly impossible to do—patience relies on the purposes of the Lord who is compassionate and merciful.

IS KIND

Maybe it's worth pointing out here that, in the Greek, the words used for both patience and kindness are verbs. In grade school, most of us learned what a verb was. A verb is an action. That's an important part of what love is. A lot of people think of love as an emotion. There are emotions that come with love, but love isn't *only* an emotion. It's a verb. It's action. It's actually doing something. In that sense, love isn't something we fall into. It requires effort and activity on our part.

They say that the best defense is a good offense. If patience is love's defense, then love's offense is kindness. This is the other side of the coin. Love doesn't only absorb hardship—blow after blow—but it also responds. It gives something in return. In return, it gives kindness.

Kindness is easy to understand. It's a word that means showing yourself useful or full of service to others. Or, to make it as simple as possible, kindness is doing good. In this, we should remember that "good" isn't defined by me, myself, and I. It's also not defined by culture and society. True goodness is defined only by God. The Bible says: "Good and upright is the LORD" (Ps. 25:8). He is good. All goodness finds its source in him, and his own character and will are what define good.

This is how love responds. A response of kindness needs two things. Paul wrote: "See that no one repays anyone evil for evil, but always seek to do good to one another and to everyone" (1 Thess. 5:15). First, kindness intentionally doesn't respond with evil. Isn't that how we often react? Someone does us wrong, so what's our response? We're going to one-up them. We're going to get even. They said *this,* so I'm going to say *that.* They did *that*, so I'm going to do *this.* Nope, that's not what kindness does. Kindness turns from evil.

Now here's the *really* hard part. Kindness doesn't just turn from doing evil and call it good. Kindness doesn't simply walk away. Rather, it figures out a way to do good: "Turn away from evil and do good" (Ps. 34:14). Kindness keeps its eye open for opportunities, or it actually creates opportunities to do good. Has your wife had a hard day and snapped at you? Yes, bite your tongue and don't respond in turn. But kindness goes the extra step and does good. Is someone in church irritating and obnoxious? Good on you for not losing your cool and telling them off. But kindness extends itself to do good. As Jesus said, "But if anyone slaps you on the right cheek, turn to him the other also" (Matt. 5:39). That's what love does. It seeks the good—the very best—for the one loved.

But we shouldn't mistake "kindness" for being nice, nicer, and nicest. Doing good sometimes hurts. When I was a boy, my twin brother did something he shouldn't have done. My dad called him out on it, and my brother responded, "That hurts my feelings." I'll never forget it; my dad immediately replied, "Sometimes the truth hurts." It's the same with kindness.

There's a simple example of this in the discipline of children. In the Bible, we read that God sometimes does that to us just like our earthly fathers: "They disciplined us for a short time as it seemed best to them, but he disciplines us for our good" (Heb. 12:10). Did you catch that? Discipline is an act of kindness—it's doing good. Dads need to remember that.

A couple years ago, I was talking to a dad whose teenage son was misbehaving. He asked me what he should do. I said, "Take his video games or his iPhone away." He was shocked at the suggestion. He didn't think he could do that because his son wouldn't talk to him and would be angry. Bluntly, I said, "You're the parent. You need to act like it." Failing to discipline a son like that isn't love, and it isn't kindness. Why? Because it's not actually for his good. That doesn't mean a dad should discipline as an outburst of rage or anger and whoop a kid. That also isn't good; it's evil, and it's not for their good. But right discipline—hard and hurtful as it can be—is actually one way to show kindness.

Patience and kindness. These two belong together. They are the defense and the offense of all that love is.

10

LOVE DOES NOT ENVY OR BOAST

FIVE YEARS AGO I got into lifting weights. It began when a good friend asked if I wanted to start coming to the local fitness center with him to blow off some steam and get in better shape while doing it! I'd never lifted weights, and I honestly didn't think I would enjoy it. Boy, was I wrong!

My friend, who had been a state champion in high school, was patient with me in both my weakness and my complete lack of know-how. He spent the first couple of months instructing, explaining, demonstrating, and correcting my form. This included teaching what the right form *is* but also what it *isn't*. A good coach does that. He knows it's important to do it correctly, but he's also aware of the common mistakes and blunders that are made. For example, on the bench press, I need to position my elbows like there's a tennis ball under my armpit, and I need to make sure the elbows don't flare out—a proper bench *is* this and it's *not* that.

DOESN'T AND ISN'T

That's a good way to think about what Paul does. He says, "Love *is* patient and kind," and then instantly adds, "it *does not* envy or boast." In fact, when you look at the list to follow in 1 Corinthians 13:4–8, you see that more time is spent on saying what love *isn't* than what it *is*.

Is that because Paul is a negative guy? No. Rather, it means that love is beyond the power of description. It can't simply be defined by what it is, but it must also be defined by what it is *not*. But, and here's where Paul gets a little fun, he's also being sneaky. Not sneaky in the bad sense, but he is giving the Corinthians something to read between the lines.

As we saw earlier, the Corinthian church was a hot mess. It was a church where there was jealousy (1 Cor. 3:3), boasting (1 Cor. 4:7), arrogance (1 Cor. 4:18), rudeness (1 Cor. 7:36), and self-seeking (1 Cor. 10:24). Well, look at what Paul writes love *isn't*. It's not envious or boastful; it's not arrogant or rude; it's not self-seeking. Ah! See what Paul is doing? He's saying, "You know what love isn't? *Love isn't you!*" I like to imagine that as they read this letter a little discomfort crept into their hearts as they realized Paul was writing about them.

DOESN'T ENVY

Have I mentioned I have a twin brother? We are identical, and yet we each have our own likes and dislikes. Growing up, my first "like" was drawing. I drew all the time! My brother? Not so much. In fourth grade, the local fire department had a drawing contest. We were supposed to draw a picture that showed why playing with matches might be dangerous. The winner won some money and got to ride in a fire engine to school. Everyone in the class was sure that I would win—I was sure I would win.

The day the artwork was displayed, my mom and dad took us down to the department. There was my masterpiece, and hanging beside it was my brother's attempt. If I recall, it showed a frame-by-frame cartoon of a baby grabbing matches and setting the house on fire. The next day at school the principal announced the winner: Michael Borg. I thought I'd heard it wrong. They must have gotten the wrong twin! But it wasn't the case. My brother had won.

The next week a bright red fire engine pulled up to our sidewalk and brought my brother to school. As it dropped him off, they turned the lights and sirens on and all the kids on the playground ran to watch him get out. Sure, it was his moment. Where was I? On the far opposite side of the playground, green with envy.

Envy is a nasty thing. We might say envy is a reaction to something we lack. Or, more precisely, it's a mental anguish caused by someone else having something we don't. Playground envy is one thing, but adults also envy. We envy people for their possessions—homes, cars, toys, and gadgets. We envy people for their attainments and skills. We envy people for their positions at work or in society. We envy people for their personalities. In fact, we find ways to envy people for anything good, happy, or joyful in their lives.

This is how Paul describes people who don't believe in Jesus. They are, he wrote, "full of envy" (Rom. 1:29). It's also how he describes people who don't have the Holy Spirit (Gal. 5:21), who don't agree with the words of Jesus (1 Tim. 6:4), and who aren't saved (Titus 3:3).

Love doesn't envy. Why? It's because the root of envy is self-obsession. Yep, a total obsession with yourself. Envy is the belief that because you are *you*, you should get what everyone else has. It's the attitude that it's criminal for you not to get everything you want—like you've been robbed of something that's yours. This kind of self-obsession then makes everyone else a rival. It's a *me* versus *them* attitude. Competitiveness might be good on the sports field, but it's not good in your personal relationships. That's the kind of competitiveness that destroys marriages and rips friendships apart.

Here's how James warns us:

> But if you have bitter jealousy and selfish ambition in your hearts, do not boast and be false to the truth.

> This is not the wisdom that comes down from above, but is earthly, unspiritual, demonic. For where jealous and selfish ambition exist, there will be disorder and every vile practice. (James 3:14–16)

He's right. Cain murdered Abel because of his envy (Gen. 4:1–7). Joseph's brothers sold him into slavery because they were envious (Gen. 37:11–28). Korah was swallowed up by the ground because he envied Moses (Num. 16:1–11). Saul grew in suspicion and hatred for David all fueled by envy (see 1 Sam. 18:6–9).

Love doesn't envy because love isn't self-obsessed. In our relationships, love is others-focused. Rather than become crippled with mental anguish, love rejoices in the good of others.

DOESN'T BOAST

Peacocks are colorful birds. They also have incredible feathers that are impressively patterned. Of course, peacocks also know they're colorful and impressive, and they don't hesitate to make a boastful display by fanning out their plumage. Their reputation is well earned. "Vain as a peacock," as they say.

Peacocks aren't the only boastful creatures. We are too. We happily make a display of ourselves—our gifts, abilities, and talents. But Paul writes that love "doesn't boast." The word he uses here is interesting. Older versions of the Bible say, "love doesn't vaunt itself." "Vaunt," that's a strange word. But it has behind it the idea of bragging or of showing off. Maybe you could think of it this way: "Love doesn't sing its own praises."

Let's slow down for a moment. Shortly before I graduated college, I had a job interview. I hoped to get work as a gas and electric meter reader. As I sat at the conference table during the interview, the supervisor told me it was a competitive market. A lot of other people also wanted the job. So, she asked me why I would be a good fit. That's always an awkward moment. You know that you have to "sell" yourself by assessing your own strengths. I mention this because there is a place to give honest assessments of yourself—being honest about strengths, talents, and even gifts.

This is different from the boasting Paul is writing about. Proving a qualification is different from an outward display of yourself for the sake of flaunting your feathers. The Pharisees—we've talked about them already—enjoyed doing this. Jesus said, "Beware of practicing your righteousness before other people in order to be seen" (Matt. 6:1). He went on to give examples like sounding a trumpet when you give to the needy. Or praying for everyone to see you. Or fasting so that you're seen by all. That's boasting. It's doing things in order to get people to sing your praises.

Paul's point is that love doesn't boast. Why? Much like envy, boasting is terribly self-centered. It's a self-interest that says, "I'm so great everyone else should have to say it. Say it together now: 'Kyle is great!'" That sounds stupid. It's supposed to sound stupid when we boast about ourselves. As Solomon taught, "Let another praise you, and not your own mouth" (Prov. 27:2). In other words, put down your feathers, you peacock.

Love doesn't need public recognition. Love doesn't need public applause. Love doesn't need public praise. Love is content to do things even when it's unseen. Love is content to do things even when it's unknown. Love is content to do things when it's unacknowledged. Love delights in anonymity. "And your Father who sees in secret will reward you" (Matt. 6:4).

Love is more than *is;* it is also *doesn't.* Love doesn't envy, and love doesn't boast.

11

LOVE ISN'T ARROGANT OR RUDE

AS WE'VE SEEN, the church in Corinth was getting a written spanking from Paul. They had lost their way and needed to be brought back with a firm hand. The words that he writes in this love chapter don't ooze with sentimentality. Rather, as he writes about what love *isn't*, the Corinthians were supposed to read between the lines. Love *isn't us*.

Within fifty years of Paul's writing this letter—which he likely did between 53 and 57 AD—another letter was sent to Corinth. It was sent to them from Rome by the hand of a man history remembers as Clement of Rome. His letter to them is the oldest Christian document outside of the New Testament. Why isn't it included in the Bible? Because Clement wasn't an apostle. He wasn't an eyewitness to the life, death, or resurrection of Jesus Christ, and he wasn't set apart by Jesus himself to be an apostle. So, while his letter is of value, it's not part of the Bible—it's not the Word of God.

Still, it is encouraging. It's encouraging because when Paul wrote to this congregation, they were having trouble with envy, boasting, arrogance, rudeness, and self-interest. Within fifty years, however, when Clement wrote to them, they were a different church! He praises them because their faith was fruitful. They were godly, hospitable, knowledgeable, and obedient. He says their young men were serious-minded, and their wives were loving to their husbands. Clement went as far to say that they deserved to be universally loved.

ISN'T ARROGANT

In his letter, Clement specifically mentions that the Corinthians were known for their humility. He says they weren't puffed up with pride. That's very different from what Paul wrote when he told them: "Some are arrogant" (1 Cor. 4:18). What is arrogance? In the last chapter, we talked about boasting. Boasting is praising yourself. It's more than recognizing your strengths, talents, or gifts, but trumpeting them for all to admire.

Arrogance is different. It's more of an attitude than it is an action. It's an attitude toward yourself. It's an attitude toward yourself that isn't very accurate. For example, it may be very accurate to say that LeBron James is one of the greatest basketball players who ever lived (sorry, I still think it's #23—MJ!). But if LeBron were to sing his own praises about how great and gifted he is, it would still be boasting. Arrogance doesn't reflect on the truth. It's a puffed-up attitude toward yourself. It would be like John Doe thinking he's the greatest basketball player even when he couldn't dribble or shoot.

Arrogance is a bad attitude. But it lies close to all of our hearts. I always laugh when presidents are asked to grade their time in office, and I'm still waiting for even one of them to say they get an "F." Actually, I'd probably be happy if one of them said, "I give myself a C-average." It's funny until you realize we all do it. We generally give ourselves a passing grade. Very few people probably think as highly of us as we do of ourselves. In fact, so difficult is it to think rightly about yourself—without a puffed-up and inflated view—Paul says it takes grace: "For by the grace given to me I say to everyone among you not to think of himself more highly than he ought to think" (Rom. 12:3).

I remember attending a funeral once for a man who was known to be hard and arrogant. Of course, the family thought of something nice to write in his obituary and engrave on his headstone. But to those of us who watched, we wondered if it would have been more honest to inscribe on the marble for all time: "Here lies an arrogant man."

But love isn't arrogant. It doesn't puff itself up. I've always tried to encourage my kids that if I wrong them in some way they should come and talk to me about it. That sounds nice. . . . until they do it! When they do, my immediate response is usually self-defense. There's an unwillingness in my heart to entertain the idea that I was wrong. We do that in all kinds of relationships. When's the last time someone gave you an assessment of yourself and the knee-jerk response was to puff yourself up and insist that you were better than their assessment? That's what Paul is talking about here. Love doesn't do that. It doesn't hide behind inflated views of self. And if it does, then the promise of God meets it: "God opposes the proud" (1 Peter 5:5). Think about that: an arrogant man is opposed by the God who is love.

ISN'T RUDE

When I was a boy and our family was invited to someone's house for dinner, I was often reminded—with severe warnings—that there were certain expectations. For instance, I couldn't turn my nose up at the food that was served or refuse to eat it. That was a tall order for a kid who was a picky eater. I had to remember to say "please" and "thank you," and I had to mind all my manners. We teach our kids those things because there are certain standards or expectations that need to be met. We don't want our kids to be rude. Unfortunately, as someone once observed—and I can't quite remember where I saw it—in our society we have an emerging renaissance of rudeness.

After writing that love isn't arrogant, Paul adds this definition to love: it isn't rude. The Greek word for "rude" is fun (*aschémoneó*). It's a noun with a prefix. Simply, it has the prefix "a-," which means "not" or "without." It really has the same meaning as the prefix "anti-." The noun that this prefix is attached to is the word "pattern," "form," or "standard." Okay, this isn't grammar class, so I'll just say it. To be rude is to be "without a pattern" or "without a standard."

When I was in the Air Force, we had a strict code of conduct. It mattered how we behaved ourselves, groomed ourselves, and dressed ourselves—nothing like some military bearing to teach a little bit of self-responsibility. This is especially drilled into you during basic training. During my third week, one of the training instructors caught me off guard. He gave me an impromptu inspection. He then yelled in my face—as instructors are apt to do—that I was a "dirtbag airman." Why? He said something was off about my uniform. He ordered me to stand in the corner and think about the standard of dress until I could figure out what was wrong.

Well . . . I stood there for two hours. Eventually, he grew more tired than I did and began having other members of my group examine my uniform. No one knew what was off. Finally, he told me. I had laced my boots improperly.

The first lace—at the bottom of the boot—went under and not over. He proceeded to yell some more, and warned me to never step out of line—to never dishonor his Air Force again.

Don't think of Paul yelling like a training instructor or pointing out some little detail. What Paul is saying is that there's a certain standard—a pattern that love follows. And to behave in a way that steps outside of that pattern—to be without a standard—is rude, and it's not love. Why? Well, to treat someone in an inappropriate way is to dishonor them. Honor is a slipping virtue in our world today. But there's something about being honorable that connects with men. Being dishonorable isn't a quality we want on top of a résumé. To be rude to someone is to dishonor that person and to be a dishonorable man.

There's an example of this from Paul. He wrote, "If anyone thinks that he is not behaving properly toward his betrothed, if his passions are strong, and it has to be, let him do as he wishes: let them marry" (1 Cor. 7:36). When Paul says "not behaving properly," he's using the same word—*rude*. Paul is saying there's expected behavior from a man toward the woman he's engaged to. That expectation is that he doesn't have sex with her.

The *only* appropriate place for any sexual experience is within a biblically defined marriage. If a man thinks he might be rude by not controlling his hormones, he should marry her. It would, in fact, be rude for him to have premarital sex. Why? Because he isn't acting in an appropriate way in that relationship. A man who does that is dishonorable and has dishonored a woman. It's why elsewhere Paul says, "Each one of you knows how to control his own body in holiness and honor" (1 Thess. 4:4). It's impossible to express love to someone through sexual immorality because it's rude.

There are patterns of behavior. There are expectations for men and women, for those who are old and those who are young. There's a standard for husbands and wives, parents and children. For example, Paul says, "Older men are to be sober-minded, dignified, self-controlled, sound in faith, in love, and in steadfastness" (Titus 2:2). Or, "Fathers, do not provoke your children to anger, but bring them up in the discipline and instruction of the Lord" (Eph. 6:4).

Those are God-given expectations for how men should behave and treat others. Love gets that. Love does that. Love interacts with others in a way that's appropriate. But rudeness is without a standard; it's without a pattern.

Love isn't arrogant or rude.

12

LOVE DOES NOT INSIST ON ITS OWN WAY

DO YOU REMEMBER that kid in school who was the self-proclaimed video game champion? You know the one I'm talking about—pale and pasty because his skin never saw natural light. He had that look . . . a Nintendo-induced, zoned-out, coma look, where he'd sit with his mouth wide open oblivious to everything around him. The only reason you knew he was still alive was because he was mashing the buttons. Yeah, that's the kid!

Remember him? If he didn't have the controller in his hand he'd be barking orders: "Press A, press B, do this, do that . . . go down that tube," or in his prepubescent voice he'd scream: "Finish him!" while Ryu delivered the final blow. However, if you didn't do things exactly his way, his exasperation would get the best of him, and he'd try to rip the controller out of your hands because no one played as well as he did. Man, he was obnoxious.

FILL IN THE BLANK

He's also the kid who would come into Paul's direct line of fire. Love, he says, "does not insist on its own way" (1 Cor. 13:5). Or, as some put it: love doesn't seek its own way. Actually, what Paul really writes isn't as specific as that. What I mean is this: the word "way" doesn't appear in the Greek (the language in which the New Testament was originally written). What it really says is something like: *love doesn't insist on its own.* Its own what? Paul doesn't say. Does that seem a little incomplete? That's because it is. The way Paul words this is probably intentional. It's to capture our attention; it's to emphasize a point. It's almost as if Paul wrote, "Love does not insist on its own [fill in the blank]."

It's a smart move. It doesn't leave room for us to try to sneak out or do gymnastics to escape what Paul is saying. The application is nearly endless. The force of it is to simply say, "Love doesn't insist on its own *anything*." And everything falls into that anything.

RIGHTS

Well, let's do a little bit of work to fill in the blank. Maybe the best place to start is that love doesn't insist on its own [rights]. Wait a second! Insisting on rights is almost as American as apple pie. After all, if it's a right, then I have a right to have my rights. Please hear me out.

Let me start with the example of Paul himself. Earlier in this very letter, he tells the Corinthians that he didn't charge money for his preaching. But here's the thing: he could have. Why? "The Lord commanded that those who proclaim the gospel should get their living by the gospel" (1 Cor. 9:14). Jesus himself commands that preachers get paid money—as a preacher, I admit that's a little awkward to write. But the Bible says it.

Paul didn't make use of that right. He could have, and there would have been nothing wrong if he had. That's the point of a "right." It's good, it's proper, it's just. Paul would have wronged no one if he had been paid for his labors, no more than you wrong your boss on payday by wanting and expecting your wages.

However, the key comes in Paul's explanation. He wrote, "I have made no use of any of these rights" (1 Cor. 9:15). Why? He says: "For though I am free from all, I have made myself a servant to all" (1 Cor. 9:19). Ding, ding, ding! Paul gave up his right to be paid as a preacher. No one took that right from him; the church in Corinth didn't take it away, and the city council in Corinth didn't either. Paul himself gave up his rights. And he actually says that's true freedom.

Sometimes we think freedom means we can do what we want. That's not wrong. It's also not all that freedom is. Freedom is also not having to do something. After all, if we must do something, it's not really freedom. Paul was free. He was free to charge money for preaching and he was free to not charge money for preaching. Paul was free to not insist on his rights. That's the freedom the gospel of Jesus Christ gives.

That's what love does. It doesn't insist on its rights. It doesn't demand that everything I am owed be given to me—from my spouse, children, friends, or even my enemies. Maybe there's no better living example of this in our daily lives than the love of a mother. From the moment a baby is conceived a mother gives up her rights—her rights to her body, energy, health, and sleep. Surrender is the high calling of motherhood.

INTERESTS

We can fill in the blank with another word. Love doesn't insist on its own [interests]. Paul wrote, "Let each of you look not only to his own interests, but also to the interests of others" (Phil. 2:4). Paul doesn't say we can't have our own interests—or that we can't give attention to things that concern us. The Bible commands us to mind our own business (1 Thess. 4:11). John says, "Watch yourselves" (2 John 8), and we're told to test our own work (Gal. 6:4). Love isn't a complete and total disregard for self.

What Paul does mean is that we need to be aware and even sensitive to the interests of others—to the things that concern them. He said this was the mind of Jesus. How? Jesus, who is the eternal Son of God, became a servant. In Jesus's own words, "The Son of Man came not to be served but to serve" (Matt. 20:28). His service was one of humble obedience leading to death on the cross. Why did Jesus live and die? He didn't do it for himself. He lived, he obeyed, and he died to serve *us*. He wasn't only interested in himself, but he gave attention to things that concerned us. He gave attention to our needs and gave himself, body and soul, for our sake: "For our sake he made him to be sin who knew no sin, so that in him we might become the righteousness of God" (2 Cor. 5:21).

Paul says that's the mind each of us needs to have "which is yours in Christ Jesus" (Phil. 2:5). In other words, this is what Jesus gives us. He takes our hopelessly self-centered minds, minds that think only about our interests, and gives us minds so that we can think about others. So that you can "count others more significant than yourselves" (Phil. 2:3). Stop for a second and think of how many problems wouldn't be problems if we learned to do that.

This is what love does. It considers other people's interests. Not in a busybody or meddling way. People have a right to privacy, and we don't get to pry into people's lives. But love takes an interest in the lives of others and the burdens they bear (Gal. 6:2), the tears they shed and their joys (Rom. 12:15), and their needs (1 John 3:17).

HAPPINESS

Let's put another word into the blank space. Love doesn't insist on its own [happiness]. We live in a society that seeks to maximize personal happiness. So much so that we determine the worthwhileness of a relationship on the basis of how happy it makes us. One day I got a call from a friend. I could tell she was choking back tears on the other end of the line, and soon it became obvious why. Just that afternoon her husband had gotten home from work and announced that their marriage was over. Why? Because she didn't make him happy anymore. We live in a society that thinks that's okay. We think it's okay for a man who made a promise "Till death do us part" to break that promise because he isn't happy.

As another example, I met a young man once who had cut off all communication with his parents. That's a nightmare come true for any dad or mom. As we talked, I found out that he ended the relationship because he thought his parents didn't want him to be happy. In fact, they wanted him to be miserable. They expected him to have a job, make some money, and take responsibility for his life.

This isn't what love does. Love doesn't seek its own happiness; rather it seeks the happiness of the beloved. Listen to what Paul wrote, "The unmarried man is anxious about the things of the Lord, how to please the Lord. But the married man is anxious about worldly things, how to please his wife" (1 Cor. 7:32–33). He isn't being critical or saying marriage is a bad thing. Marriage is a very good thing. He was making a simple observation. A husband cares about his wife and family, and he wants to provide for and care for their well-being.

We could probably go on and fill that blank in with all kinds of other words. Love does not insist on its own opinions, preferences, desires, ideas, gain, wants, needs, popularity, benefit, and so on. But I think you get the point: love doesn't insist on self. So many problems among husbands and wives, parents and children, people in the church, and friends come from our ability to be self-seeking. But love doesn't turn the eyes inward; it turns the eyes outward, not to self, but to others.

Love doesn't insist on its own way.

13

LOVE ISN'T IRRITABLE OR RESENTFUL

MY FAMILY AND I took a camping trip a few years ago. Wanting to avoid as much traffic as possible, we left late in the evening. As we made our journey, the weather got stormy. We arrived at our campground a little after midnight in the middle of a torrential downpour. My wife jumped out to help direct me into our spot—a job she had never done before. As I slowly backed the camper up, I found that I wasn't moving. I hit the gas a little harder, and still I wouldn't budge. I crept forward a bit and again put it in reverse. The same thing happened. I jumped out to see what was happening. It was then I discovered our 27-foot camper was crunched up against a tree and our awning was shredded.

As soon as I saw it, I threw a temper tantrum of toddler proportions. I'm glad the darkness hid me from sight, and the rain and thunder drowned out my yelling. I lashed out at the closest thing to me: my wife. Like a real jerk I hollered: "How could you let this happen? This is all your fault! Are you blind? How didn't you see the tree?" It wasn't fair, it wasn't nice, and I shouldn't have done it.

The next morning I was still cranky. She and the kids tiptoed around me like they were walking on eggshells. I decided to call my dad. I thought, "If anyone will understand me it's going to be him." I told him what happened, thinking he'd commiserate with me. He didn't. Rather he chastised me in a firm but gentle way. He said, "Those things happen. I remember when we were on vacation and everything seemed to go wrong. But what I remember more is all the fun we still had. Don't be angry, don't blame your wife, and go have fun with your family." Let's just say before the fun started, I had a lot of apologizing to do.

ISN'T IRRITABLE

If there are sins men are especially prone to, anger is probably one of them. There is a kind of anger that isn't wrong. If there wasn't, then God would be wrong: "Behold, the name of the Lord comes from afar, burning with his anger" (Isa. 30:27). Even Jesus expressed anger. We read in the Gospel of Mark that parents were bringing their little children to Jesus. The disciples, annoyed by this, tried to push them away. We're told Jesus was "indignant" (Mark 10:14). That's a strong word—he was furious. This kind of anger (the anger of God and of Jesus) is actually an expression of love. It's the kind of anger that responds to injustice and unrighteousness. We too can be angry for those reasons, but we need to be careful: "Be angry and do not sin" (Eph. 4:26).

It's probably safe to say that *most* of the anger we feel isn't *that*. I'm not always good at practicing it, but when I get angry, my default is to assume I'm feeling a righteous anger. Usually, it's not. It's not a righteous anger to be angered by the dog who barks incessantly or to be angry about the mess the kids make. Literally, they touch something, and it just gets messy. It's not good anger when I'm fed up with someone or annoyed by their quirks and personality. Look, let's be square. It's not righteous anger when traffic is slow or when the team I'm cheering for loses. No, those are all examples of what James calls the anger of men: "Know this, my beloved brothers: let every person be quick to hear, slow to speak, slow to anger; for the anger of man does not produce the righteousness of God" (James 1:19–20).

It's also not loving. Paul says love "is not irritable" (1 Cor. 13:5). The idea is that love doesn't easily get upset. It doesn't have a short fuse. But, like the God who is love, love is "slow to anger" (Ps. 86:15). Why? Why is love contrary to an outburst of anger? Again, it has to do with how self-focused anger is.

Just before I sat down to write this chapter, my daughter and I ran an errand. It was pouring rain. When we got back into the truck and she climbed from my seat to hers I said, "Don't get your muddy shoes on my seat." What did she do? She got her muddy shoes on my seat. What did I do? I got angry. In my own head I immediately thought, "How could she do that to *me*?" When I snapped at her, I learned that she hadn't even heard me over the sound of the truck and didn't even think about her muddy shoes. No law of justice was broken, no principle of righteousness was violated. In fact, as it was, no mud even got on my seat. A darling seven-year-old girl had been absent-minded—that's what seven-year-old girls do!

My irritability was me-centered. I assumed she intentionally ignored me, I refused to consider the circumstances, I blew things out of proportion, and I made a snap judgment. I turned into myself. That's not love. That's selfishness; that's irritability.

ISN'T RESENTFUL

Most people know Charles Dickens's most famous character from *A Christmas Carol*: Ebenezer Scrooge. And prior to his encounter with the four ghosts, we probably also remember his character. He was a penny-pinching miser.

Scrooge was the kind of guy who pored over his ledger. He had every single penny that he owned and every single penny that was owed perfectly accounted for. He probably even knew by memory the exact column and row where the debts were written.

Scrooge's bookkeeping is the perfect example of what love isn't: love isn't resentful. What does it mean to be resentful? Usually, we understand it as feeling anger toward being wronged. But what Paul means here is that love doesn't keep a record of wrongs. Love isn't in the business of bookkeeping—it doesn't keep a running score.

Now, like patience there's something we need to see here. When Paul says love doesn't keep a record of wrongs, there's an assumption. What is it? The assumption is that those we love will wrong us. When my wife and I were dating, we got along like two peas in a pod. We once said to each other, "I don't know what we'd ever do to not get along." Ah, the ignorance of youthful bliss. Then reality hit. I don't always do right by my wife, and my wife doesn't always do right by me.

You can apply that to any relationship. Parents wrong their children, and children wrong their parents. The people we worship with and fellowship with in church are not always going to do what they should toward us. Friends? Friends can blow their mouths off—they can tell secrets, betray confidences, and sometimes do horrible things. Any relationship you have with another person will inevitably, certainly, and unavoidably result in them sinning against you. And you're no better. You will sin against your spouse, parents, children, friends, and enemies. It happens. That doesn't make it right. It's still wrong. But it happens.

What Paul writes is practical for every relationship. When wronged, love doesn't open the ledger and make sure there's a written record: "So-and-so sinned against me at 5:42 p.m. on January 30th." It doesn't do that. Love keeps no record of wrongs. Instead, love forgives.

Peter once asked Jesus, "How often will my brother sin against me, and I forgive him? As many as seven times?" (Matt. 18:21). You see what Peter wanted to do? He thought he was being a pretty good guy. He'd give his brother seven chances but then . . . well, he wasn't so sure. We read that Jesus said, "I do not say to you seven times, but seventy-seven times." Then he went on to tell them a parable. It was a story about a man who owed his master 10,000 talents. A talent was about twenty years' worth of work. Add it up. That's 200,000 years' worth of wages—about $10 billion today. When he couldn't pay, his master forgave his debt. The servant went home and on his way ran into a man who owed him 100 days' wages. The servant grabbed him, choked him, and demanded that he pay what was owed. When the master heard what the unforgiving servant did, he had him thrown into jail until he could pay his whole debt. Jesus said, "So also my heavenly Father will do to every one of you, if you do not forgive your brother from your heart" (Matt. 18:35).

Love doesn't tally up all the wrong that has been done. It forgives. Peter must have gotten the point. Years later he wrote, "Above all, keep loving one another earnestly, since love covers a multitude of sins" (1 Peter 4:8). That's the tremendous strength of love. It can cover a multitude of sins. But when love can't do that, when love can't overlook an offense, it can also lovingly confront those who have sinned. Love doesn't have to be an ostrich with its head in the sand. Love is big enough to be able to confront and seek reconciliation with those who have wronged it.

Now, I know there are people who have been very seriously sinned against. Tragically, abusers and enablers twist what the Bible says on this topic. Their condemnation will be just. The victims need a lot of care, sensitivity, and individual attention in those circumstances. Often, in those cases, a lot of outside help is needed. Hopefully, our churches are places where they can receive help.

But for the sake of simplicity let me set *those* situations aside. Many of the ways you are sinned against daily—by your spouse, parents, children, fellow church members, and friends—aren't that. It's still sin and still wrong. But what is love's response? It doesn't keep a record of wrongs.

Love isn't irritable or resentful.

14
LOVE DOESN'T REJOICE IN WRONGDOING

FROM TIME TO TIME when I was growing up, I'd go to the doctor for a checkup. Many kids do. Parents want to make sure that everything looks good and is working well. They run you through a bunch of tests, checking your eyes, ears, and throat. There is also the knee jerk reflex test. Or in the fancy medical world, it's called the monosynaptic reflex.

As a boy, that was the one that amazed me the most. I'd sit on the table with my legs hanging over so they could swing. Then the doctor would take a little rubber hammer and he'd hit the spot just below my knee cap.

Automatically, my leg would kick out. Apparently, I passed the test.

THE REFLEX OF LOVE

The knee jerk reflex test is intended to make sure there's no problem with a sensory nerve. Amazingly, it only takes about 50 milliseconds from when the doctor taps the knee to the movement of the leg. What happens in those milliseconds? When tapped on the knee, the thigh muscle stretches and sends information to the spinal cord. That information is then sent back and the thigh muscle contracts. The simple test shows that your neuromuscular system is working—you've got good reflexes!

Love has a reflex. Just like your leg moves automatically when hit with a rubber mallet, love also does something in response to something. What does love do? What is love's reflex? It rejoices: "[Love] does not *rejoice* at wrongdoing, but *rejoices* with the truth (1 Cor. 13:6). Rejoicing is the reflex, it's the reaction.

To rejoice means that you feel or express joy or great delight in something. We can rejoice in trivial things like when our favorite sports team wins the Super Bowl, or we rejoice in important things like the birth of a son or daughter. One of the great things about Christianity is that rejoicing is important. Some people think that Christianity is a killjoy. Maybe you'd be surprised to find out that rejoicing—to express joy and delight—is actually commanded by God: "Rejoice in the Lord always; again I will say, rejoice" (Phil. 4:4).

The Christian always has a reason to rejoice. When the disciples were arrested and beaten for preaching the gospel, "They left the presence of the council, rejoicing that they were counted worthy to suffer dishonor for the name" (Acts 5:41). These bloodied and bruised men were delighted that they could suffer for Jesus Christ.

It matters what causes us to rejoice. We need to have pleasure and delight in the right things. One of the problems of sin is that it gives us wrongly directed rejoicing. School-age boys are a good example of what Paul is writing about here. That's because there's a juvenile attitude that thinks it's really cool (and funny) to push the limits. Teenage boys can be rude, perverted, disrespectful, boastful, foolish, and disobedient. They and their friends delight in it—high-fiving, laughing, and egging each other on. Paul wants us to know how love rejoices: it doesn't rejoice at wrongdoing but with the truth.

AT WRONGDOING

Love doesn't rejoice at wrongdoing. That may seem obvious. I also imagine that at first glance most of us would agree. After all, when is the last time you read the headline "Four People Murdered" and felt delight? I'm guessing that doesn't happen to you. Paul wants us to know that love never delights in sin. The thing is, there are a lot of not-so-obvious ways we often do that.

We delight in wrongdoing when we *encourage* others to sin. One of my best friends growing up had a stash of *Playboys* provided to him by his dad. Is that what a dad is supposed to do? No! Fathers are to encourage their children to walk in a manner worthy of the Lord (1 Thess. 2:12). Unfortunately, some dads are really good at encouraging sin in their children's lives—teaching them with words or by example. Love doesn't do that. Love doesn't encourage others' wrongdoing.

We can delight in wrongdoing when we *celebrate* sin. Someone I know had a friend getting married. That's usually a reason to celebrate, but in this case the friend was getting married to another man—a same-sex wedding. I was asked how, as a friend, that person could respond in love. That's not an easy situation but the question has an easy answer. By God's design, marriage is for one man and one woman. It's wrong to have a same-sex marriage. A friend who loves cannot celebrate others' wrongdoing.

We can delight in wrongdoing when we *affirm* other people's sins. Today, many people think that affirmation is love. This is especially true with LGBTQ+ issues. We're often told that to not affirm their lifestyle—chosen or not—isn't loving. We're accused of hate speech and some suffer the onslaught of cancel culture. But understand this, a Christian's refusal to affirm these things isn't because we're motivated by hatred. It's because we're called to love, and love cannot affirm what God calls sin: "Though they know God's righteous decree that those who practice such things deserve to die, they not only do them but give approval to those who practice them" (Rom. 1:32).

We can delight in wrongdoing when we take *pride* in others' sins. I knew a young man who had a bit of a rebellious streak. At school, he talked back to teachers, was a jerk to the weird kids, and gained a bad reputation. When the school addressed his parents about his behavior problems, his dad actually beamed with pride. He was happy his son had gained the reputation he had. Love doesn't take pride in others' wrongdoing.

We can delight in wrongdoing when we *benefit* from other people's sins. The Bible tells us it matters how we use our words. No, the Bible isn't concerned about creating a list of four-letter words, but it does say we can't lie, flatter, slander, or gossip. To be a gossip is sin. But how often do we benefit from other people's gossip? We're glad when they tell us things they know, reveal secrets, or talk about things that aren't any of our business. Do we stop them? Nope! We've got itching ears, and they do a good job scratching them. Love doesn't benefit from others' wrongdoing.

We can also delight in wrongdoing when we *tempt* other people to sin. The Bible says, "Fathers, do not provoke your children to anger" (Eph. 6:4). Part of Paul's concern is that some fathers can be overbearing in rules and expectations;

they can be uncaring and unsympathetic to their children. What's the result? Their children can become exasperated and even angered. The way a dad relates and interacts with his children can actually become a way to tempt them toward sinful responses. Love doesn't tempt others to wrongdoing.

We can also delight in wrongdoing when we *fault-find* other people's sins. A guy once told me that he believed God had put him on earth to point out how wrong others were. He was really good at it. He could turn over every stone in the things people said and did and tell them how they had gone wrong or failed. How many wives feel the burden of a harsh husband who nitpicks them to death—everything they do, everything they say? The husband gets some gleeful happiness from pointing out her weaknesses, deficiencies, and sins. Love doesn't fault-find others' wrongdoing.

There's another way we can delight in wrongdoing. It's twisted logic, but it's also twisted delight. It's when we're actually glad when other people do wrong or fall into sin. This is especially a temptation with people we regard as our enemy. You've probably heard someone say, "I wouldn't wish that on my worst enemy." Well, often that's not true, and we do wish the worst on our enemies. I knew a man who tragically ruined his marriage and family because of adultery. He had done a wicked thing. Some of his ex-wife's friends used it as an opportunistic moment to gain personal victory: "I told you not to marry him. I'm just glad we figured out who he really is." His wrongdoing became a point on their side of the scoreboard. King Solomon wrote: "Do not rejoice when your enemy falls, and let not your heart be glad when he stumbles" (Prov. 24:17).

The point of Paul is large. Wrongdoing—wherever it is or however it is expressed—is never, ever a source of delight for love. Your attitude toward what is wrong is a test of whether or not you love.

Love does not rejoice at wrongdoing.

15

LOVE REJOICES WITH THE TRUTH

WE'VE SEEN A LOT about what love does and what love doesn't do. As it was said earlier, love is an action. It's an activity. In that sense, we don't "fall in love" as the poets like to write. We make the decision to love. We choose to love.

Sometimes we really need to remember that. I was meeting with a young couple engaged to be married, and I asked them the question, "When you don't feel in love with your significant other, how do you still love?" I probably could have asked the question in a foreign language—or even strung together nonsensical sounds, and it would have had as much effect on these two. It had never entered into their minds that they might not always feel the way they did in that moment.

Well, it happens. It happens with husbands and wives, it can happen with parents and children, and it can among our friends and church family. We don't always feel like we love them. In those moments we need to remember that love is primarily an act of the will—daily deciding to love and to do good to those in my life.

THE AFFECTION OF LOVE

But does that mean love has no emotions? Of course not. Emotions or affections accompany love. How do we know? I think a pretty solid answer comes from a simple appreciation for who we are. God has created us. All of us. He has created our body, and he has created our soul. He's created us with a will, intelligence, and emotions. That's right! God has created our emotions—and no, they weren't given to women only. While people experience and express emotions differently, our emotions are part of what makes us human.

When you read the Bible, you find that some of the most prominent men were emotional men. The mighty man of war, David, who also wrote some of the psalms, expressed all kinds of emotions, especially in his songs. Paul, Silvanus, and Timothy wrote to the Thessalonians and said, "But we were gentle among you, like a nursing mother taking care of her own children. So, being affectionately desirous of you, we were ready to share with you not only the gospel of God but also our own selves, because you had become very dear to us" (1 Thess. 2:7–8). Even Jesus himself had an emotional life of compassion, amazement, anger, grief, and joy. That's why I'm not impressed (and neither should you be) by men who think there's some manly virtue in being stoic. That's to deny a fundamental part of who God created us to be.

So what is the emotion of love? We often associate it with the sweaty palms, beating heart, or butterflies in the stomach. But biblically, the main emotion associated with love is delight. Remember, love has a reflexive response. That reflexive response, as I said earlier, is rejoicing—or delight. Our relationship with God expresses itself in delight (Ps. 37:4). The love of a husband to a wife is found in delighting in companionship and physical pleasures (Prov. 5:19). The love of a parent to a child, to other Christians, and to friends is a mutual delight in one another.

Of course, love's delight also means that there are other emotions that accompany love. The psalmist delighted so much in the law of God that he experienced sorrow and grief when that law was broken (Ps. 119:136). The love we have for others in the church leads us to be jealous over them with a godly jealousy (2 Cor. 11:2). We are to be so delighted in loving God that, comparatively speaking, we hate: "If anyone comes to me and does not hate his own father and mother and wife and children and brothers and sisters, yes, and even his own life, he cannot be my disciple" (Luke 14:26).

But the main emotion, the primary affection of love, is that of delight.

WITH THE TRUTH

The word "truth" stands on the other side of "wrongdoing." Here, it means what is right and what is good. To paraphrase what Paul says, love doesn't rejoice in vice, but it rejoices in virtue. Love finds delight and pleasure in the truth. The apostle John wrote, "I have no greater joy than to hear that my children are walking in truth" (3 John 4). That's the reflex. When love meets with truth—with what is good and right—it rejoices. *It can't help but rejoice.*

That's important for the way we love others. It's important for how we interact with our spouse, children, people in the church, and friends. It means that love will always praise the good of others. Instead of trumpeting their faults and failings, love shines a spotlight on what is good. This isn't flattery. Flattery is an insincere praise. Insincerity is wrong. Therefore, love doesn't rejoice in it, and the Lord will cut off flattering lips (Ps. 12:3). Love, however, genuinely expresses praise for that which is good in the one loved. For instance, in words that apply to a godly mother and a wife, we read, "Her children rise up and call her blessed; her husband also, and he praises her" (Prov. 31:28).

It also means that love will seek out the good in others. We've already said some people delight in fault-finding. They dig deep to figure out where others have gone wrong. They search and search and search for what is bad. Love delights to seek for the good. We've already seen that the church in Corinth was a disaster. People there were argumentative, boastful, impatient, envious, and on and on. There was a lot wrong. But Paul began his letter not by saying, "Here's what I've found that's wrong about you," but he started by saying, "I give thanks to my God always for you" (1 Cor. 1:4). He found something good in them. That's what love does. It delights in the truth, and so it searches for it.

It also means that love will help cultivate good in others. This is true, for example, of dads. They're not to provoke their children to anger, but what are they to do? Paul says, "Bring them up in the discipline and instruction of the Lord" (Eph. 6:4). It's what people in the church are to do toward one another. As the author of Hebrews said, "Let us consider how to stir up one another to love and good works" (Heb. 10:24). Our loving responsibility to those around us is to help them grow in what is good. It's to encourage, build up, and strengthen one another (1 Thess. 5:11). That's what love delights to do.

It also means that love will correct the bad when it's needed. No, not the nitpicky way of trying to stick it to people or take them down a notch. But a word of loving rebuke and correction. Sometimes that's what's needed. It's needed in order to push back the bad and bring forward the good.

This is why, for example, parents are called to discipline their children: "Whoever spares the rod hates his son, but he who loves him is diligent to discipline him" (Prov. 13:24).

In some ways, we can say that what is being written here is our entire responsibility to our neighbor. It's as if Paul has gone through various qualities of love—patience, kindness, not envious or boastful, not arrogant or rude, etc.—and as he comes to write these words, they're a catch-all. I can imagine Paul thinking, "Love is so much more than what I've already said. Here, this is the broadest way I can say it." Love toward our neighbor praises, seeks, and cultivates all that is good in the eyes of God. Love doesn't rejoice in wrongdoing, but rejoices with the truth.

16

THE "ALLS" OF LOVE

I REMEMBER SITTING in a conference room once for a workplace meeting. We were all eager to get out for the day and hoped that the boss would keep it short. After a bit, he said, "Okay, one more thing." And . . . you probably know the drill. That one more thing extended another thirty or forty minutes. I thought it was never going to end. I hope that's not what you're thinking at this point in the book.

I said in the previous chapter that, when Paul wrote that love "doesn't rejoice in wrongdoing, but rejoices with the truth," that was a catch-all. Almost like Paul knew he had to wrap things up, but he wanted to make sure that we really got the point about what love toward our neighbor *is* and *isn't*. Is there anything left to say?

Yep, there is! In quick succession Paul says a lot more: "Love bears all things, believes all things, hopes all things, endures all things" (1 Cor. 13:7). But he isn't being repetitive or trying to wear us down. So, what is he doing? Maybe it's useful to think about it this way. He's giving a final motivational speech to love. Okay, that might not be the best way to think about it. Personally, I always groaned when a motivational speaker came to our school. They're usually full of half-digested advice and cheap platitudes. That's not what I mean.

Rather, think about the way a general commands his troops in the heat of battle. Some of the greatest speeches have come in war—Washington, Bonaparte, Churchill, and George S. Patton. In a few words, leaders must persuade the hearts of men under the weight of the immensity of the challenge to take the field and never retreat—to face every challenge and every power with unflinching resolve whether they live or die. That is, I think, what Paul is doing.

Paul understands that the preceding qualities of love are an immense challenge. They aren't frothy sentiments. They're not really meant to be embroidered on a pillow. Rightly understanding and applying these to our relationships—marriage, parenting, church, friendships, enemies—is a tall order. It's not easy. It's not for the faint-hearted. It's not for those with wobbly knees. In keeping with the picture above, it's actually a declaration of war—

to war against self and selfishness for the good of others. Therefore, the field must be taken and there must not be retreat. So, like a commanding general, Paul motivates, "Love bears all things, believes all things, hopes all things, endures all things."

BEARS ALL THINGS

When we think of "bearing," we think in terms of carrying something. It sometimes has the added emphasis that the thing being carried is heavy. For instance, in the Bible we read: "Bear one another's burdens, and so fulfill the law of Christ" (Gal. 6:2). Burdens . . . they're heavy. We feel weighed down and even crushed by them. Christians help each other bear those burdens. They climb under them together, put their backs into it, and help those who are weak carry the things that weigh them down.

In a similar way, there's a burden that comes with love. Every quality of love that has been pointed out comes with tremendous weight. It's like lying on a bench in the weight room, and you've got the barbell in your grip. Paul adds one plate after another to each side and then says, "On the count of three, lift." Ugh! It's so heavy. Paul says, "Love is patient and kind." Do you know how hard that is? Do you know how burdensome that can be? It's not easy. And the one who tries to love his wife, kids, and friends like that is going to find it difficult.

In those moments that tiny voice starts to speak. "Be patient? Nah, that's too hard. Give it up. Be kind? Forget it. Get even." But Paul won't have it. In the face of the question, "Can I carry the burden of love?" Paul reminds us: "Love bears all things." Love is willing to bear any burden, shoulder any difficulty, suffer any suffering for the sake of the one loved. As Jesus said: "Greater love has no one than this, that someone lay down his life for his friends" (John 15:13).

BELIEVES ALL THINGS

When I worked at summer camp, one of the activities we did with our campers was the "trust fall." You've probably heard of it and maybe you've even fallen! We would have a camper get up on a picnic table, blindfold them, and then we'd ask them to fall straight backwards with the promise that we would catch them. In my years of doing that with hundreds of campers, I never met one who wasn't a little nervous.

That's because it's not always easy to trust. Trust requires us to put faith in something or someone else. Trust sometimes requires us to believe something without fully understanding it. Trust sometimes means we need to believe something or someone despite evidence pointing to the contrary. Trust sometimes forces us into a situation that is as serious as life and death. It's not always easy to trust.

That's true of love. Remember, Paul had told the Corinthians that love was the most excellent way. When at a crossroads—one being the road of love and the other the road of non-love—Paul is saying, "Always choose the way of love." That sounds nice until you realize what the way of love requires. What does it require? It requires complete self-denial. It's not an easy road. The road of selfishness is smooth, straight, and well-paved. The road of self-denial is rocky, muddy, steep, and difficult. Love requires you to walk that road. Paul said, "Love does not envy or boast." That requires getting over myself. It means I can't be self-obsessed. It means I don't get to toot my horn no matter how much I think I deserve it.

As we walk that road, we'll constantly be bombarded with the question, "Is it really better to be selfless than to be selfish? Is this actually the best road? Do you really believe it's best to do this?" Again, Paul will have none of it. In the face of the questions, he says: "Love believes all things." Or, to put it this way, love always chooses to trust that love is the best way. No matter what that means, no matter if we fully understand it, no matter the evidence to the contrary, *love* trusts that love is always best.

HOPES ALL THINGS

Hope. It's a great word. Even better than the word is the idea. Hope is confidence. It's confidence about something we don't have yet. Hope is confidence in the present about the future. A farmer is a man of hope. In the spring, he tills and plants with the hope that at harvest time he'll have a good crop.

True hope is the property of a Christian. No one knows for certain what will happen tomorrow. We don't know what will happen in an hour. But God hasn't left his children in a vast sea of uncertainty. No, he's given us promises. And because God can't lie (Heb. 6:18), those promises are guaranteed. That means whatever happens here and now, one day I'll get what is promised. I may not have it today and I may not get it tomorrow, but one day I will. What do we do in the meantime? We patiently wait. We wait for the day when we will get what we hope for.

Hope is important for love. That's because it constantly plants good in the lives of other people—our spouse, children, friends, and enemies. Now, in our perfect world, when we do good to others, we'd like to think that they will immediately do good to us. In our ideal world, when we love others, they would love us in return. But we don't live in an ideal world. We live in a real world. Often, the good that we do to others—the love we show them—isn't reciprocated in the moment. Sometimes not for a day, years, or even a lifetime.

As love sows the seed of good in other people's lives and sees no fruit, you will be assaulted by doubt. It's easy to be pessimistic about the present. After all, what's the use of loving my spouse when all I get is the cold shoulder? But Paul again will have nothing of it. In the face of doubt, Paul says, "Love hopes all things." Love lives in the present with an immovable confidence for the future. Might the one to whom we do good never do good or love us in return? Yes, that's possible. However, love still plants what is good, certain that one day every promise of God will prove "Yes and Amen" (2 Cor. 1:20).

ENDURES ALL THINGS

My son and I enjoy working out together. He's only ten, so right now it's really enjoyable for me. I can outdo him in anything. But he's a tough guy. Sometimes we dedicate the end of our workout to a test of endurance. One day, we decided to see how long we could dead hang. I went first. It didn't go well. I could try to make excuses but there wouldn't be much point. My son, on the other hand, did great. He grabbed the bar and hung perfectly still. At first he made faces at me, pretended to yawn, and hurled competitive insults. When he passed my time I thought for sure he'd just drop, but he didn't. He kept hanging. His whole body started trembling and sweat was pouring down his red face. Realizing he was in it to win it I cheered him on. I started saying over and over again, "Endure! Endure!" Finally at almost six minutes, he crumpled to the ground, exhausted. But he had exhausted himself using every ounce of energy he had.

Amazingly, to love people in the way that Paul directs us isn't always met with gratitude and excitement. People can resist love. They can set up hurdles against it. They can make it difficult to love them. They can even become outright hostile and angry. I talked to a heartbroken dad once. His son made a life-altering decision and, in so doing, deeply hurt his parents. He decided he didn't want anything to do with them. The dad reached out, but each time he did, he got his hand slapped. His son grew angrier and angrier, more and more bitter.

People don't always want to be loved in this way. In those moments, there's a compelling urge to quit. To give up. To stop. But Paul won't have any of it. Here's his final push: "Love endures all things." The love that he has described here is a love that is not and cannot be overthrown by any opposition. It's a love that is committed to doing good to another no matter the consequence. And to continue doing and persevering in it because it is invincible. Love doesn't quit. Love doesn't give up. It keeps going no matter the difficulties.

Love is patient and kind. Love does not envy or boast. It is not arrogant or rude. It does not insist on its own way. It is not irritable or resentful. It does not rejoice at wrongdoing, but rejoices with the truth. Love bears all things, believes all things, hopes all things, endures all things (1 Cor. 13:4–8).

There is only one time in human history where these qualities were perfectly bound together by the "alls" of love, united in perfect harmony. That place was the cross of Calvary. "This is my commandment, that you love one another as I have loved you" (John 15:12).

17
CONCLUSION

LOVE NEVER ENDS, but this book must.

I began by saying that we live in a noisy world. There are a lot of voices around you that are trying to tell you what love is. It's everywhere—philosophy, psychology, mathematics, science, pop culture, pornography, and so much more. Those voices can be loud. What we need is a voice that breaks through the chatter and perversions, and clearly, authoritatively, and conclusively defines for us what love is. We need a definition that doesn't depend on culture, place, or time. Or, to put it another way, I need a definition of love that doesn't depend on me. My preferences. My opinions. My personality. My habits. We need a love that is beyond ourselves.

I am convinced that the voice we need to hear is God's voice in the Bible. I have put forward in these chapters the Bible's description of love. The Bible gives the most perfect description imaginable. You could search the world 10,000 times over, and you wouldn't find an idea of love that is as incredible as this.

What could you *add* to improve it? What could you take *away* to make it better? Can Hollywood? Or music? Can pop psychology? Or science? Can philosophers, poets, or politicians? Or fairy tales or pornography? Who will offer a more complete, fuller, or more perfect description of this something we call love?

What is love? It is something that finds its source outside of ourselves and completely independent of us. That's because God is love. Love is the most excellent of all things. It's something that is bound and directed by the good and pleasing will of God as he's expressed it in his law. It's something into which we were created with God and our neighbor, and that sin brought to utter ruin. But God in a demonstration of love gave his beloved Son, and, by the Holy Spirit, has found a way to restore love to those who believe in the promises of the gospel. Love is at the heart of every significant relationship in this life. Its qualities shine with the brightness of absolute and total selflessness, and it delights itself in giving for the good of another. It's something that bears all things, believes all things, hopes all things, and endures all things.

Love is the lightning flash of the Lord. A fire of supernatural power kindled by God himself that shines most brilliantly and purely in the face of Jesus Christ.

GRASSMARKET PRESS

GRASSMARKET PRESS is named for the square in Edinburgh where many Reformed Presbyterians (also known as Covenanters) were martyred for preaching Jesus Christ's reign over Scotland and all earth. Though many lost their lives, their witness for Christ endures. Grassmarket Press aims to help Christians know, practice, and stand for their faith.

THE BEDROCK SERIES aims to provide clear, concise books on Christian doctrine and life from a Reformed and Presbyterian perspective.